TO OUR READERS

Different, but the same

Change for the sake of change makes for shock and chaos. Ask anyone who's ever come home in the dark to rearranged furniture in the living room. But in the media world, change is the prudent response to an ever-evolving landscape. The "platforms," as those in the business like to call them, are many, and they keep growing—smartphones, tablets, digital newsletters and action alerts, YouTube channels and who knows what else.

Despite the proliferation of devices that "deliver content," most media pundits say the publication you are holding has a bright future. *Island Journal* has produced the finest long-form reading—profiles, analysis, history, fiction, poetry—and the most beautiful imagery that only an insider like the Island Institute can bring you, an organization that cares about Maine's islands and coast.

What we publish annually is not quite a magazine, not quite a book. But with elements of both, *Island Journal* is poised to stand tall in the crowded media environment, the experts say. People still want to leisurely read and savor the stories we tell, and feast on the rich imagery that completes the picture.

And speaking of standing tall: this, the 31st annual publication, is a different shape. It will not stand symmetrically next to the 30 other *Island Journal*s many of our readers have on their shelves. And this is where change, even for the sake of change, comes into play.

Magazines and newspapers regularly pay consultants to revamp the look of the publications—not necessarily to fix a design that's broken, but often to freshen up a look that's grown tired. We've gone to the wider, slightly shorter shape for the 2015 *Island Journal* in part to freshen up our look.

And we did it without hiring a consultant.

Our designer, Eric Wayne, says with this size and shape, the mostly horizontal photographs in our stories can be better displayed. Scott Sell, a triple-threat as video producer, photographer, and writer, has taken the helm as art director, succeeding the much-esteemed Peter Ralston, the Island Institute co-founder who decided to step aside. Scott scoured the coast and islands for the photos and art that make the publication sparkle, choosing only the best from among many.

We're excited by what's inside. Our stories, photographs, and art will take you to an island off the Irish coast and another in Denmark; to the past, when World War II turned the Casco Bay islands into fortresses, and to the same period when peace-loving Quakers came to Vinalhaven; to early 20th century photos documenting life on the islands and coast and the 21st century photos shot off the back of a fishing boat; to the more recent past and the 10-year anniversary of the economic phenomenon that was credit-card lender MBNA; and even to the distant past—literally, eons ago—in an explanation of Maine's beach stones.

We look forward, too: the work being done to keep island housing affordable; the Island Institute's Fellows service program, which puts recent college grads on islands and in remote coastal communities; islanders farming on land and in water, raising lamb and oysters; and Stonington, a town on the edge. And where else would you find the tale of a couple of boys riding the falling tide with a seal?

If you've picked up *Island Journal* for the first time, you need to know that it is produced by the nonprofit Island Institute, founded in 1983 and dedicated to supporting the 15 year-round island communities and remote coastal communities in Maine.

So if you're new to our publication, thank you for trying us. If you're a longtime reader, welcome back. And maybe choose a new shelf for this *Island Journal,* and many more to come.

—*Tom Groening, editor*

ISLAND JOURNAL

The Annual Publication
of the Island Institute

Volume 31

Exchange Informs Local Action

From Thailand and Cambodia to Denmark and Alaska, common bonds emerge

BY ROB SNYDER

≈

Why travel anywhere but to Maine's islands and along its coast? After all, our communities inspire. They inform a way we all might live, conscious of environmental boundaries but gladly sharing within them what we have in common with each other.

Yet despite this bounty of local experience and leadership, an increasingly global world pulls us outward. The movement of people and the climactic shifts we induce intersect and connect with Maine's island and coastal communities. The value of our harvests rise and fall as global commodities. Real estate prices climb according to local as well as international trends; lending practices ease and restrict. And another energy company seeks space in an already territorialized ocean.

Witnessing these outward forces—and, more important, understanding them—is critical to what we do at the Island Institute. And that is why we look outward as well as inward.

Far from home, on brackish Songkhla Lake in Thailand, a dozen fishermen are trying to rebuild their fishery. It is a place largely ungoverned; the rise and fall of shrimp aquaculture in this region destroyed their mangroves and left them without income. Gliding across wind-chopped water, the canoe's roughly hewn planks chafe while we try to talk above a Briggs and Stratton engine running wide open. We discuss familiar topics: how to generate more profit per fish, how to curb overfishing, how to attract and retain young people, how to formalize and expand communal conservation measures.

These fishermen are creating a community fishing territory where none existed. It is both a conservation area filled with homemade artificial reefs and an education tool. A floating house on the lake is open to all who wish to learn about the conservation practices. In exchange fo :

learning, visitors can access the conservation area.

These fishermen are selling directly to consumers, too; a restaurant along the primary north-south artery in southern Thailand generates pride and profits. Their solutions resonate. And in the Gulf of Thailand, Muslim fishing communities fight the siting of an LNG terminal. They find inspiration in the stature and impact of fisheries advocacy groups in Maine.

≈

High over Sitka Sound, looking down at an island town perched on the edge of the Pacific, we talk of the increased need for policies that create more workforce housing. The discussion turns to a lack of political representation among the island communities of Southeast Alaska. Examples from home that are shared include *The Working Waterfront* newspaper as a source of regional identity and the Maine Islands Coalition as a vehicle for amplifying island voices. These solutions, created on the coast of Maine, inspire and motivate action far from home.

A group of Maine islanders sought inspiration on Samsø Island in Denmark. In doing so, energy conservation methods that can be applied to Maine islands are gleaned, and a sense of common cause emerges. By happenstance, our group crosses paths with a meeting of representatives from small European island communities. We join 50 or so people, meeting in the round, and spend the day sharing challenges and solutions. Those from Maine who volunteer tirelessly are reinvigorated by being with people who do the same to sustain island communities in the Atlantic and Mediterranean. The result: all recommit to the hard work of making positive local change.

≈

World travel transports and grounds. As day descends

deplane in Cambodia. I've not been here before, but an overwhelming olfactory moment transports. The smoke of unwashed coal drifts up through the palms into a smoldering red sky. For a moment, a thousand memories flood back from experiences lived nearby, in Yunnan, China. A blink and I'm back to the present, asking what will be learned that will be of value back in Maine. This is the optic through which my time is evaluated.

The social enterprise model of economic development adopted by Cambodians is truly inspiring. Cambodians who began their careers as minority partners in foreign-owned businesses now own the hotels we stay in, the restaurants at which we eat, and even the tour company that guides us. This development scheme pervades post-Khmer Cambodia and is pulling people out of poverty. Perhaps some aspect of this idea could work in Maine, where we rely heavily on the economics of a lobster industry propped up by hyper-abundance. How will we diversify into shellfish and kelp aquaculture?

Through exchange, we become more resilient. Our networks grow and we share "what works" and what doesn't. It is a productive plagiarism that can speed innovation.

We are beyond the days when the thought of replicating solutions in their entirety had currency. However, we may still find that one piece of a solution that can travel with us, back to Maine. Alaska, Italy, Cambodia, Thailand, Denmark, the US Virgin Islands—in each place I've traveled this year, the local context has been different, sometimes radically so. But when listening closely, one hears echoes of old stories, of similar solutions being brought to shared challenges, locally and practically, the world over.

Certainly we can and must learn through travel. To think otherwise would be to succumb to an echo chamber of our own making. ♦

Rob Snyder is president of the Island Institute, publisher of Island Journal.

Making Salt Hay While the Sun Shines

North Haven lamb, once prized on the Boston market, could be again

STORY AND PHOTOS BY SCOTT SELL

After nearly a year, Maya, Issie, and Velma still refuse to be sheep. They have acted like goats since their first days on the farm, and most days you can find the three of them with the goat herd, walking through the woods and taking naps in the cemetery. The couple of times Doreen has tried to put them in with the other lambs and ewes for a sleepover—to get them adjusted to being together—they cry their hearts out to go back to their adopted goat family or to be taken inside to watch TV on the sofa.

Life with farm animals is nothing if not chaotic. There is never a dull moment. And like most farmers, Sam and Doreen Cabot's work days on North Haven's Foggy Meadows Farm begin and end in the dark, most of their time devoted to their Katahdin sheep and Boer goats. Today, they have almost 80, in various states of pregnancy, hoof injury, and sickness.

Along with the reluctant sheep, a mink has just killed one of the ducks. A ewe has complicated mating season by snubbing her suitor. Neighbors have suddenly stopped in to buy jams and frozen meat from Doreen's farm store. Island deer have been eating the garden's tomatoes as midnight snacks. And one of the young goats has gotten his head stuck in the fencing again. Even daily chores—

which have to be done more or less the same way—can be different, given the weather or animal temperament or ferry schedule.

~

One thing is a constant at Foggy Meadows Farm, though: the sheep and goats feed throughout the year solely on grass and hay from several island fields that Sam mows, "teds"—or spreads out for drying—and bales himself.

Driving over to the north shore to bale the last cut for the season in late September, Sam points out several fields he hays, many of them old family farms, which amount to about 90 acres scattered around the island.

"That's what you call a 'Tootsie Roll'," Sam says, pointing out a long line of hay bales, bunched up end to end without the ubiquitous white shrink-wrap. "They sit out in the fields all winter and the inside stays nice and dry."

Hay on North Haven is mostly wild orchard grass, with a fair amount of clover and purple vetch. Sam and Doreen like it because it's a fine-grain hay, very soft for the animals, especially the lambs and kids. A majority of the hay that's sold on the mainland has been seeded, and, according to Sam, if it hasn't been harvested at exactly the right time, it ends up being too coarse to eat.

"They won't touch it when it's like that," Sam explains. "They claim that if you take a bunch of hay and squeeze it in your hands and it pricks you, that's the same feeling the animal would have in its mouth."

Like most jobs on an island, haying is a time-sensitive process and occupies much of Sam's time throughout the summer and fall. He starts cutting in June and tries to finish by the beginning of August, before the hay matures. This allows the protein content to stay intact. Early on, before up-to-the-minute weather forecasts on the TV and Internet, Sam lost whole fields at a time when passing rainstorms suddenly drenched his tedded piles. When that happens, the protein leeches out and it turns to straw.

Now, after waiting nearly a week to get a few sunny days in a row, the hay on the north shore has dried out, and Sam hitches a red Hesston 530 hay baler on the back of his John Deere. It's a round baler, capable of almost vacuuming up the hay as Sam drives the tractor slowly in long lines. And then, at the push of a button, the baler bundles the hay

Sam and Doreen Cabot with their goats and Maya, Issie, and Velma, the sheep SCOTT SELL

with twine and spits out a
perfect round bale. Last year, Sam made about 240 round bales, a record.

"That's the side you want to be on, having too much versus too little," Sam says. "It's like firewood. You want extra; you don't want to run out. Those animals stay hungry."

Even when there's plenty of new pasture grass to eat, the sheep and goats don't bulk up on it because it's mostly water and doesn't fill up the "rumen" section of their stomach. It's the hay they need to help their digestive process. They need that dry matter to stick to their bones.

The animals have preferences on their hay, too. They especially love the hay that comes from along the edge of the water, like down on Amesbury Point, south of the house. That's where "salt hay" grows: grasses that have ocean air constantly blowing over them, leaving a continuous layer of salt. Sam says that it'll take almost a year for the animals to go through a salt lick that's kept in the barn: they're getting all the minerals they need from the salt in the hay.

"The animals tell me that it's good," Sam says. "When they dive into it, you can tell."

⁓

The high salinity and iodine content of the grasses on the shore give prepared lamb a unique flavor and is considered to be a delicacy. It's
what French chefs call *agneau de prê-salé,*
or "salt meadow lamb," particularly those raised on marsh meadows on the northern coast of France. On North Haven in the mid-19th century, it was no different.

North Haven was just stone walls and wide-open pasture then, perfect for raising sheep for both wool and meat, which quickly became mainstays of the island's economy. Among the 71 island farms of the time, all but one kept sheep. And at one point, sheep were the majority: the 1850 Agricultural Census reported 2,156 sheep on North Haven, approximately double the human population on-island at the time.

And North Haven lamb was so highly sought after that it was a specialty in many high-end restaurants in Boston and New York. Large boats would come up the coast and, in addition to the plentiful island produce, they would load countless sheep to carry to Boston, where North Haven lamb was its own commodity on the Boston Market.

"We're hoping to regain some of that specialty with our animals," Doreen says. "It would be nice to have that kind of niche, to have people excited about island lamb again."

In the fall, the Cabots sold all of their ram lambs and

Sheep at Frank Waterman's farm, circa 1920
COURTESY NORTH HAVEN HISTORICAL SOCIETY

some of their ewe lambs to be slaughtered for customers, mostly their island neighbors, who either bought whole animals or sides. Nebo Lodge, an inn and restaurant on the island, ordered 10 whole lambs that will be served as chops for dinner and sausage for breakfast during the upcoming season. And there's a possibility that they'll start selling their goat meat—often called *chevon*—to grocery stores in Portland, if there's a market for it.

But they are reluctant to expand too much. For now, they're trying to keep it simple.

"We're not a very big farm and it's only the two of us," Sam says. "If it ever got really popular, we'd have to start expanding to more pasture, more fencing, more, more, more. How the hell would we keep up with it?"

~

On a warm fall morning, Sam is busy putting eastern-facing doors back on the barn and reinforcing the small animal shelters and hay houses, buttoning everything up for the oncoming cold and snow. The sheep watch with great interest as he measures and hammers and drills.

"When there's no pasture to feed on in the winter, these critters go through a round bale in three days," Sam says, laughing at them. "They'll eat from morning until night and get as round as butterballs."

Doreen comes down the hill to feed the goats, with Flossie the corgi and Maya the black sheep trailing close behind. Maya sidles up against Doreen's thigh and gets a head scratch before Doreen runs her hand along the sheep's spine.

"It's not rocket science," she says. "We usually go by body tone. If they're energetic and their ears are up and they're bright-eyed, then you're doing it right. You just have to hang out with them so they can tell you."

Although the winter allows Sam a break from haying and gives Doreen a chance to catch up on canning and crafts projects, they're looking forward to warmer weather: after breeding ended in November, they're expecting to welcome over 60 lambs and kids by the end of the spring.

And the big news on the farm is that the Cabots have new cattle, two Hereford steer, after finding an ad in *Uncle Henry's* classifieds. It's going to be a lot of work. A lot of new fencing will have to be put up and a new shelter will have to be built. But they're excited. Their family farm started when they got their first Hereford calf, Uh-Oh, in 1979, and they haven't had cattle since 1997. The couple's five-year-old granddaughter Emma thinks the new steer should be called Dumb and Dumber. They, too, will feed on island hay. ♦

Scott Sell is the media specialist at the Island Institute.

2014 Katahdin sheep class photo
SCOTT SELL

Deer Isle-Stonington Fellow Ian Watkins working with Long Island students on a service learning project. KENDRA JO MARSH

Island Fellows:
A 'Peace Corps for the Islands'

Fellows reverse Maine 'brain drain,' provide extra hands

BY ABIGAIL CURTIS

The board funded the Fellows program in 1998, and the following year the first two hardy souls were placed on Monhegan and in Casco Bay.

It was the kind of blustery January night that was so cold the snow squeaked, but inside the Islesboro Central School gymnasium, the athletes playing basketball were starting to work up a sweat.

The moms, dads, and neighbors sitting on the bleachers stomped and clapped as the Islesboro Eagles boys team began to coalesce and take the lead over the Jonesport-Beals Royals. The home team's shots arced sweetly into the net. Teenagers wandered around the perimeter of the gym, socializing and buying paper bags of salty popcorn. A wide-eyed baby got handed around the bleachers, getting cuddles and coos from the islanders. And a young woman with long brown hair hunched over the scorebook, ignoring all off-court distractions as she marked shots and fouls for the referees to use later as the official record of the game.

That scorekeeper, Kendra Jo Marsh, is an Island Institute Fellow who has lived on Islesboro for more than a year. The 23-year-old from landlocked Buckhannon, West Virginia, recently graduated from the University of Connecticut with a degree in human development and family studies. She came to Islesboro to work on a project connecting island families and children to mainland resources, building a database to support islanders' access to services they need.

"Families don't come off the island very often for services," she said. "If families aren't coming off and providers aren't coming on, kids start to fall behind."

Like many of the 102 Fellows who have been placed on Maine's coastal and year-round island communities in the last 15 years, Marsh has found a multitude of ways to weave herself into the pattern of Islesboro life. The college and master's degree graduates have served in 21 different communities, among them Islesboro, the 14-mile-long, narrow island in upper Penobscot Bay. There, Marsh teaches country line dancing at the community center to an enthusiastic crowd, most of whom are retirees. She coaches Ultimate Frisbee, works at the "Kidz Club" after-school program, and helps an autistic boy with his homework. And she keeps the books for home and away games, spending long hours on the school bus as the basketball team travels to schools around the state.

Her contributions have been invaluable, said the Islesboro school's athletic director, Jack Schlottman, who

Islesboro Fellow Kendra Jo Marsh shows off donations to her Martin Luther King Day food drive. KENDRA JO MARSH

remembers other Fellows from past years also sharing their talents with the island community.

"Would you want to ride seven hours to Eastport and back on a school bus? No!" he said emphatically. "But she does it. She's doing this stuff people take for granted. The Fellows program is wonderful. We always find slightly different things for them to do."

Sometimes, he mused, the Fellows don't leave. And that's a boon to island communities struggling to keep their populations up.

"They come. They fall in love with somebody, and the island as well, and the next thing you know, they're here for life," Schlottman said.

∾

Although the Island Fellows program is carefully structured these days, it wasn't always so, according to Karen Burns, the community development director for the Island Institute. In the late 1990s, a board member first imagined sending young, energetic college graduates to the islands to address community needs. The board funded the Fellows program in 1998, and the following year the first two hardy

souls were placed on Monhegan and in Casco Bay.

"It was an experiment," Burns said. "Over the years, it's become a much more systemized program. Before, it was more the idea of an extra set of hands. It's been a trial-and-error process."

In 2004, the Island Institute Fellows program became part of AmeriCorps, the national service organization started during the Clinton administration. Now, the graduates accepted into the highly competitive Maine program get benefits such as room, board, a $15,000 annual stipend, and a $5,500 education award after completing their service. They are chosen by both the Island Institute and the community where they will be living and working, and they are assigned a specific project.

Recently, the program has been earning accolades around the country. It won a 2014 Sustainable Homes Index for Tomorrow (SHIFT) Sustainability Award and was featured at the SHIFT festival in Jackson Hole, Wyoming, an annual event that celebrates the future of conservation. Additionally, it was highlighted as an innovative education program in a national publication that showcases AmeriCorps State and Volunteer Generation Fund Programs.

But in the early days, the first Fellows felt like pioneers.

Kathleen Reardon at work in 2013
JOCELYN RUNNEBAUM

"It was definitely a bit of a struggle. They didn't really know what to do with us," Kathleen Reardon, a geographic information system (GIS) Fellow on Islesboro from 2000 to 2002, remembered. "They weren't sure what to expect of me."

The Rhode Island native, then a 22-year-old graduate of Williams College who loved islands, remembers those first days as being both challenging and rewarding.

"I moved out at the end of October, that time when everyone hunkers down," she said. "My parents let me have the cat. They said, 'We have each other. You can have the cat.' I learned to be by myself. I went on a lot of walks."

She also spent a lot of time going to all the community meetings she could find, listening to what was said and figuring out ways that she could help. At one cemetery committee meeting, she learned that islanders had just had a report done on arsenic levels in the island wells. Reardon offered to compile that data into a map. It was a hit, and she ended up teaching a couple of GIS classes at the high school and in the adult education program. She continued to go

opinions," she said. "It made me very flexible. It made me able to talk to almost anyone, and find some common ground."

Her experiences as an Island Fellow ultimately reaped benefits in her current career as a scientist with the Maine Department of Marine Resources.

"If you ask the wrong questions, the fishing community is very quick to judge," Reardon said. "On Islesboro, I lived in their community. I taught their kids. I learned how to talk to fishermen."

～

Since the program began, Island Fellows like Marsh and Reardon have worked in libraries, schools, historical societies, town offices, and land trusts. They've counted fish, marked storm drains, cataloged books, developed school programs, increased access to affordable housing, assisted in public health services, and winterized drafty island houses. Along the way, they've often decided they like island life.

Like many of the 102 Fellows who have been placed on Maine's coastal and year-round island communities in the last 15 years, Marsh has found a multitude of ways to weave herself into the pattern of Islesboro life.

on long walks, collecting more data as she tromped over Islesboro's fields and through its forests, and made more maps.

Reardon became part of the community, making more friends and pitching in wherever she could. She was an extra set of hands working on the town's comprehensive plan, and began a lobster sampling project. She listened to the fishermen as they painted buoys and passed the time talking about gear. Along the way she learned much about the island—and a lot about herself.

"I am really close to my family. I have lots of cousins, aunts, and uncles," Reardon said. "All of a sudden, I was put in a place where I didn't know anyone. They didn't know me. I had to learn to listen, see where I could help, and adapt and fit into the community."

Those skills were important parts of what Reardon and her cohort called "the Maine island Peace Corps."

"It's about putting recent graduates into a situation where they have skills that can help, but they aren't imposing their

More than half of the Fellows have stayed in Maine, Burns said, and a third still live and work in islands and coastal communities.

"We're really working as a reverse braindrain for the state of Maine," she asserted. "We're bringing in young, bright people who have fallen in love with the state and are staying. It's been a side effect that we weren't anticipating but which has really been great for the state of Maine."

She knows what she's talking about. Burns, who grew up in suburban Massachusetts, came to Vinalhaven to do a performing arts fellowship at the school from 2003 to 2005.

"I thought this was a one-year adventure," the bubbly Island Institute staff member said. "I stayed on, became a drama teacher, became the high school English teacher. I stayed for multiple reasons. One was that I fell in love with the school and teaching, and that was not something I intended to do. Second, I fell in love with the community. Thirdly, I fell in love with a generational fisherman. And this is where my life is."

Elder Care Fellow Maddey Gates interviews David Cooper on North Haven. MADDEY GATES

Experiences similar to Reardon's have occurred up and down the coast. Joy Sprague, the longtime Islesford postmistress, sounded practically effervescent when she described what the Island Fellows have meant to the Cranberry Islands. At the very beginning, Sprague said she was curious about how the program would unfold for the town of Cranberry Isles. When Marine Stewardship Fellow Jesse Minor and his girlfriend Rebecca Larkin came in 2002 to Islesford, they assuaged any doubts. They jumped right in to island life, with Minor joining the volunteer fire department, organizing a first responder and CPR course, and giving fiddle lessons to the islanders.

"That was just a wonderful experience. They really had the bar raised," Sprague said, adding that the duo even got islanders to count baby lobsters once a month at low tide in a grid they had set up. "It was amazing. The quality of the work and the energy they put out, bringing people together. Getting people excited about getting out at six in the morning to count lobsters! They not only helped in the lobstering industry, they were also such vital and important members to the community, contributing on so many levels."

Sprague said that while Maine islands get an injection of life in the summertime, it is particularly nice to have year-round residents.

"They really become part of the fabric of the community, as people who just really get it. They give and also take with them a real vital experience," she said. "I can't say enough good words. I commend the Island Institute for seeing this possibility, to be able to look into the future and see that this was something that could be very important, and very valuable to the community."

On Swan's Island, Candis Joyce has been advisor and mentor to several Fellows. As the island librarian, Joyce supervised some who worked in the library, and helped others who worked for the historical society

"It's a great program," she said. "I think it's the best thing the Island Institute has come up with. It's amazing what these young people do." Though she believes the observation was made by Island Institute founders Philip Conkling and Peter Ralston, Joyce says the best way to describe the value of the program is: "Islanders have no lack of ideas or enthusiasm or vision. We don't have enough people to get it done." Fellows bring the energy and dedication to the work.

Joyce notes that not every Fellow is a good fit, but the

program is self-selecting in certain qualities.

"I've always had fairly self-motivated people here. If they're not self-motivated, I don't think they can make it on these little islands," she said. Still, some arrive nervous, and some arrive very comfortable in the sudden immersion into an insular, isolated community.

"It's the whole range," she said. Many with outgoing personalities take on work outside their formal roles, Joyce said, remembering one Fellow whose presence after-hours at the library would bring people in to read and talk.

The mentoring is personally rewarding, Joyce said.

"I've learned as much from the Fellows as they have from me, if not more," she said.

Her only regret is not being able to keep in touch with past Fellows. "I wish I had more contact with them," she said, naming some of the earlier participants who now have families.

≈

Back at the Islesboro basketball game, many in that island community cheering in the bleachers said they hoped Marsh

might like island life enough to stay when her fellowship is done. The islanders have welcomed her, opening their hearts and doors to the girl from West Virginia.

"The community on Islesboro reminds me so much of my community back home," Marsh said during a break in the action. "The number of people who feed me! People have just taken me in."

Sprague, the island postmistress, said it's sad when Fellows leave the Cranberry Isles at the end of their stint—but she loves to see them get off the mailboat when they return to visit.

"It's like family," she said. "You miss them when they're gone. But sometimes living on an island forever is not something that's going to work out. You just feel very fortunate and very blessed when people do come here and share a little bit of themselves." ♦

Abigail Curtis lives in Belfast and covers the Waldo County beat for the Bangor Daily News. *She spent many happy childhood days on Bowman's Island and Williams Island in Casco Bay, and worked for a memorable summer on Islesford.*

Kendra Jo Marsh, back row on the left, with Islesboro Central School students
KENDRA JO MARSH

DIALED BACK IN TIME

The carved and polished past on Maine's beaches

STORY BY DANA WILDE // PHOTOS BY PETER RALSTON

Twenty thousand years ago, the snow was deep in Maine. Really deep.

It had been snowing over northeastern North America for about 60,000 years. Not much of it was melting. Snowfall after snowfall built up, packing the layers into ice and more ice. By about 21,000 years ago, a mile-and-a-half-thick layer of ice covered this part of the world, extending over mountains and easterly over the ocean as far as 180 miles from the present coastline. Geologists call this the Laurentide Ice Sheet. The rest of us, unable to do much more than scratch our heads about that much ice, just call it a glacier.

That much ice was heavy. It pushed down on the land underneath, depressing it hundreds of feet lower than it is today. Between about 12,000 and 20,000 years ago, the atmosphere began to warm and the glacier retreated as the ice age known as the Wisconsin period of glaciation came to an end. By around 16,000 years ago, the coastline was starting to show, and by 14,000 years ago the tops of Cadillac and other mountains were poking out.

We say the glacier "retreated," but this is a little misleading; more accurately put, what happened is that the glacier melted from its margin back inland. The ice itself plodded seaward the whole time, even while it was melting and breaking off in chunks (as glaciers are doing now in Alaska and other parts of the world). As the weight of the ice diminished, the land sprang back up. By 10,000 to 12,000 years ago, our lowland areas were clear.

A lot of rubble was left.

Receding glaciers leave all sizes, shapes, and conditions of rock—churned up, scarred, abraded. Just to give a few geological examples: There's *till*, which is silty, sandy rock debris; the bits ground up underneath the glacier are called *basal till*. Accumulations of soil and rocky material left by the glacier are called *moraines*. Sand and gravel deposits from melted water flowing in tunnels are called *eskers*.

Much of the material that makes up till, moraines, and eskers is hundreds of millions of years old. The glacier was just the most recent form of processing. In fact, Maine's coast began to take shape in its present jagged form when wandering land masses collided around 430 million years ago. A fragment of continental land (or *terrane*) called Avalonia—which was connected with land that now makes up parts of Europe—plowed into the proto–North American continent, or Laurentia.

In the slow-motion collision, sedimentary, igneous, and metamorphic rock that was already there turned up from the ocean bed and folded over and under. As hundreds of millions of years churned by, the continents continued to drift, until what's now the Atlantic Ocean opened up around 1.7 million years ago. Periods of glaciation over the next million and a half years sculpted the rocks and stones we see now, from the sandy beaches of southern Maine to the cliffs of Monhegan, mountains of Mount Desert, and Washington County coast.

EVIDENCE IN ROCK

The evidence of these ancient forces is everywhere in the rock, if you know how to look, and among the most alluring of its smaller bits are the smooth cobblestones and pebbles you see piled and crowded together on some beaches.

Naturally polished, intriguingly marked beach stones, as they're often called, are found worldwide. In Maine, they're less numerous on the sandy southern shore, but more abundant up through the rockier Midcoast to Penobscot Bay and Downeast. The most well-supplied beaches are often tucked into an island or coastal cove, many times

THESE CLINKING, CLATTERING COLLECTIONS
OF CRACKED AND BROKEN ROCK ARE THE JUNK
WHITTLED DOWN THROUGH THE EONS . . .

between bedrock outcrops that frame the strand. This means, as Maine Geological Survey writers observe, that waves washing up the "pocket beach" can't move the stones very far to either side, where they could otherwise be washed out to deeper water.

Instead, the stones are rolled again and again up and down the beach by the waves, tides, and storms. These clinking, clattering collections of cracked and broken rock are the junk whittled down through the eons—from the geologic folding (a component of *orogeny*, the processes of deformation of the Earth's crust) set up in the Avalonia collision, through to the glaciers, and finally into our Holocene geologic epoch, in which the stones are chipped round and polished by the relentless friction of water, waves, and each other.

The larger ones, suitable in past centuries for paving streets and finishing buildings, are called cobblestones. Smaller ones are pebbles—defined by geologists as stones measuring between 4 millimeters and 6.4 centimeters across. They're often difficult even for geologists to readily identify, in part because they're made variously of all three different basic kinds of rock: igneous (solidified from magma, such as granite and basalt); sedimentary (solidified by massive, long-term pressure, such as sandstone and limestone); and metamorphic (chemically changed by tremendous heat and pressure, but not melted, such as gneiss and marble).

In her book *Beach Stones*, Margaret Carruthers pictures stones so finely detailed they seem almost to be works of art. A 400-million-year-old metamorphic stone found on North Haven is lined with a tangle of white jags that Jackson Pollock would have appreciated. Another from Vinalhaven is a trapezoidal chunk of gray quartzite shot through with a thick line of white quartz that formed when hot water ran into a rupture in the sandstone and sealed the different quartz materials. One from Brimstone Island, which lies roughly between Vinalhaven and Isle au Haut, is a smooth, shiny, elongated piece of brimstone, a basaltic rock.

Pretty stones are free for the taking on some beaches; jewelry-makers, recognizing the natural artistry, scavenge for them to make necklaces and even earrings when suitably matched pebbles can be found.

BEACH-STONE BEACHES

Where are the best beach-stone beaches in Maine? Some are well-known, such as Jasper Beach in Machiasport, which has good examples of the "storm berms," or ridges of stones thrown up by storm waves. But stone jewelers like Barbara Fernald, of Islesford, and Anita Roelz, of Woolwich, decline to name their favorite collecting beaches.

"I see myself as a steward of the places I choose my

stones," Roelz said in reply to the question. The stones, she said, are a natural resource, which can be abused.

Indeed, the rangers of Acadia National Park keep a close eye on the stone beaches there, where Monument Cove, Little Hunters Beach, and Seawall are particularly prone to beachcombing for stones.

Law Enforcement Field Ranger Chris Wiebusch said recently that during the summer, warnings—and sometimes violation notices—are issued fairly often to people trying to carry off pieces of the beaches.

"Animals live in the rocks" in their own little beach ecosystems, Wiebusch said, and in any case, "the beach isn't an art gallery."

"It's prohibited to take any resources from the park," he said.

And that includes not only pebbles but larger items. Wiebusch said rangers once stopped a person from loading a huge slab of granite into his car on Cadillac Mountain. And some years ago, when the federal Transportation Security Administration stepped up its routines in the Hancock County–Bar Harbor Airport, the park started receiving calls from TSA officials reporting stones—sometimes bags of them—stowed in people's luggage. The rangers had to drive to the airport, collect the confiscated stones, and return them to the shore.

What's the allure, exactly?

Well, no doubt it's the aesthetic attractiveness of the stones, as the success of Barbara S. Fernald Jewelry and Roelz's Circle Stone Designs, among many others, attests.

But the visual beauty seems to be surficial, to steal a term from the geologists.

Roelz described her stone collecting as a process undertaken in "places that have interesting energy," a phrase that might hold a clue to the fascination for the stones. She said that in more secluded coves she detects a "different kind of energy . . . coming from a whole different part of the Earth," especially when she comes upon stones of "deep green" (whose colors result from the presence of iron minerals formed in oxygen-poor environments).

Such stones are "energy-enriched," Roelz said, adding: "It dials you back in time."

For indeed, when you pick up these perfectly polished and rounded stones, you're holding in your hand Earth's ancient past—12,000 years past, to the melting of the glacier and the grinding of the stones; to 21,000 years ago, when Cadillac Mountain slept deep beneath the ice; to 80,000 years ago, when the Wisconsin glaciation began; and much further back, to the hyper-ancient collision of Avalonia and Laurentia.

On Maine's beaches, you can touch the carved and polished past that lay for eons deep beneath the glacier.

Dana Wilde is a former English professor and newspaper editor who lives in Troy in northern Waldo County. The Other End of the Driveway *is a collection of short essays gathered from his Amateur Naturalist columns that have appeared in several Maine daily newspapers.*

Sources for this article include the Maine Geological Survey's Explore Maine Geology and Geologic Site of the Month reports; Margaret W. Carruthers's book Beach Stones *(Abrams, 2006); Andrew M. Barton's book* The Changing Nature of the Maine Woods *(University of New Hampshire Press, 2012); and carefully selected online sites, such as Geological History of Jamestown, Rhode Island, and Gulf of Maine Council on the Marine Environment, to help clarify and detail information.*

Vessels berthed at one of the Long Island navy wharves
COURTESY NATIONAL ARCHIVES COLLECTION

World War II left a big footprint on Casco Bay islands

STORY BY EDGAR ALLEN BEEM
PHOTOS BY SCOTT SELL

The great concrete bulwark of Battery Steele on Peaks Island is covered in earth and weeds and graffiti. The maw of the old gun emplacement stands dark, dank, and toothless, its 16-inch battleship guns removed a lifetime ago. On the face of the fortification someone has painted the words "American Heartache" in garish blue and pink letters.

Standing forlorn and neglected in a landscape of cattail and bittersweet populated mostly by raccoons and beavers, the abandoned artillery fortification, 18-inch-thick steel-reinforced concrete with a 300-foot-long tunnel down the middle, has the look and feel of an ancient ruin.

Kimberly MacIsaac, a Peaks Island native and former director of the island's Fifth Maine Regiment Museum, conducts guided tours of the island's military structures.

"This was our playground growing up," says MacIsaac, steering a golf cart into the cavernous battery. "This is where we hung out, in the forts."

The great guns at Battery Steele, with a range of 26 miles, were meant to protect the Maine coast from Popham near Bath to Kennebunkport, but they were never fired in anger. When they were fired, however, everyone on the island knew it.

"They were test-fired with about three-quarters of a charge," says MacIsaac. "You could feel the vibration all over the island. A few windowpanes would break. My aunt

There were 58 military structures on Peaks alone, ranging from gun emplacements and watchtowers to range-finding bunkers, fire-control posts, barracks, and searchlight bases.

Kimberly MacIsaac in front of Battery Steele on Peaks Island
SCOTT SELL

told me she was making spaghetti sauce once when the guns were fired and it splattered all over the kitchen."

Seven decades later, it would be hard for most people to imagine that during World War II, Peaks Island—and, indeed, all of Casco Bay—was a hotbed of military activity. There were 58 military structures on Peaks alone, ranging from gun emplacements and watchtowers to range-finding bunkers, fire-control posts, barracks, and searchlight bases.

World War II left a heavy footprint on some of the islands in the form of abandoned buildings, bunkers, and bases. Some have become eyesores, some have been renovated for new uses, and some are treated as local landmarks, but all are present and physical reminders of a history that should not be forgotten.

COASTAL DEFENSE

The coast and islands of Casco Bay are encrusted with the remains of old forts meant to defend Portland Harbor and the bay against all manner of enemies, foreign and domestic. One of the most prominent, the truncated octagon of Fort Gorges on Hog Island Ledge in the middle of the harbor, dates to the Civil War, but it was not completed before that war ended. Many of the forts along the shore, from Fort Williams in Cape Elizabeth and Fort Preble in South Portland to Fort Levett on Cushing Island and Fort McKinley on Great Diamond Island, date to the late 19th and early 20th century, but they were pressed into service during World War II, often updated with new artillery and antiaircraft guns.

In 1942, military reservations were installed on Cape Elizabeth, Peaks Island, Jewell Island, Long Island, Bailey Island, and Chebeague Island. By 1944, the US Army Coast Artillery Corps had 1,753 enlisted men and 130 officers assigned to defend Portland Harbor and Casco Bay. Nine hundred of those soldiers were based on Peaks, outnumbering the 700 islanders.

Military history is everywhere on Peaks. As Kim MacIsaac's golf cart bumps along the island's back roads, she points out the overgrown remains of searchlights and watchtowers, generator buildings and gun emplacements. Here, a former army barracks has been resurrected as a summer cottage. A veritable mansion has been constructed atop Battery Craven, which once housed a pair of six-inch guns with a 15-mile range. There, a mine casement facility known locally as "Big Daddy" has been turned into a cottage. And a range-finding station called "Little Momma," once hidden inside a cottage, now stands naked and alone overlooking the cold North Atlantic.

During the war, large areas of the bay were off-limits to fishermen, access to the seaward side of Peaks Island was severely restricted by fences, gates, and guardhouses, and even the shore was forbidden.

"Dirt was mounded up in a berm," says MacIsaac, pulling over on Seashore Avenue. "You couldn't get out on the rocks."

In World War II, the enemy was out to sea. German U-boats patrolled the Atlantic in deadly packs. In 1940, 4,407 Allied ships were sunk in the Atlantic.

THE SOUTH PORTLAND SHIPYARD

The United States did not officially enter World War II until December 8, 1941, the day after the Japanese attack on Pearl Harbor. But the war came to Casco Bay a year earlier when the shipyard in South Portland began building ships for the British.

"Portland was an exciting place during the war," says

"Little Momma," a range-finding station on Peaks, housed a telescope used to locate targets for the two anti-motor torpedo boat batteries located adjacent to it. SCOTT SELL

historian Joel Eastman. "There was just so much going on. People came from all over the country to work in the shipyards."

In 1940, the Todd-Bath Iron Shipbuilding Corporation opened the East Yard on the South Portland waterfront. In 1941, the US Maritime Commission called for a second shipyard, run by the South Portland Shipbuilding Corporation and referred to as the West Yard. In 1943, the two yards merged as the New England Shipbuilding Corporation.

The first British ship was launched from the East Yard in March of 1942. The last Liberty ship was launched in October 1945. Between those dates, some 30,000 shipyard workers built 266 Liberty ships in South Portland for the war effort.

In a chapter in *Creating Portland*, on Portland during the Depression and World War II, Eastman, emeritus professor of history at the University of Southern Maine, describes how the war pulled the city and the region out of economic decline by providing work. The population of Portland grew by 10,000 between 1940 and 1950.

With the influx of soldiers, sailors, and shipyard workers, Portland became a pretty rowdy liberty port as well. Eastman records, for example, that in March of 1943 Portland police criticized navy shore patrol for not helping to break up fights among navy men. A few days later, 1,500 shipyard workers rioted at a Portland theater when a striptease show ended unexpectedly.

But Eastman writes that "By the fall of 1944, the greater Portland area had adjusted to the impact of the shipyards, the army, and the navy, three and half years after their arrival."

Sitting in Becky's Diner on the Portland waterfront some 70 years after the fact, Eastman assesses the military history of Casco Bay by observing, "The navy is more important than the forts, because 'Destroyer Atlantic' was in Portland throughout the war. Every vessel in the Atlantic fleet came to Portland during the war."

NAVAL OPERATIONS

Commander Destroyer Force, Atlantic (ComDesLant) chose Casco Bay as its base during World War II because it offered protected anchorage close to North Atlantic convoy routes. Captain George Stewart, a retired US Navy captain and marine engineer who grew up spending summers on Peaks Island, has posted a four-part report entitled "Going Ashore: Naval Operations in Casco Bay During World War II" on the Naval Historical Foundation website.

To date, Stewart's research has identified 808 ships that visited Portland during the war, but the daily comings and goings of naval vessels, as well as ships from South Portland on sea trials, created levels of marine traffic in Portland Harbor and Casco Bay that would be unimaginable today. During one week in August of 1944, for example, 539 ships arrived and 558 ships departed. In comparison, during one week in November of 2014, just 70 vessels—fishing boats, ferries, tugs, and tankers—arrived in port.

Stewart remembers tagging along with his uncle Harry Wallace as he piloted army transport boats between the harbor and island forts. He recalls the bay being incredibly crowded and polluted with oil slicks everywhere along the shore.

"We did not have access to the waterfront on the seaward side of Peaks," says Stewart. "That was cordoned off."

Not only were the big guns of Battery Steele mounted on the back shore of the island, but a sophisticated network of submarine nets, minefields, hydrophones, and magnetic submarine indicator loops on the ocean floor monitored sea traffic and controlled access to Casco Bay. Though none of the harbor-defense guns in Casco Bay were ever fired at an enemy, the threat from the sea was real. And despite the elaborate anti-sub defenses laid out around Casco Bay, on April 23, 1945, German submarine U-853 managed to sink the USS EAGLE, a patrol boat towing targets for navy bombers off Cape Elizabeth. Fifty-four of the 67 crewmen were killed.

The two primary focuses of naval operations in Casco Bay during World War II were training and refueling. One of the few vestiges of navy training is a rusted steel box that sits on the shore of Little Chebeague Island. Designed to simulate a ship's engine room, the steel box was the classroom of the Navy Firefighting School.

"In the last two years of the war, they trained 1,500 sailors in shipboard firefighting," says Erno Bonebakker, a Portland resident and Chebeague Island summer resident who is writing a history of World War II on Casco Bay.

While the brick and concrete forts dotting the shore are visible reminders of the army's coastal defense operations, relics of naval operations are more subtle—unless you know where to look.

LONG ISLAND FUEL ANNEX

The entire waterfront of modern-day Long Island from Ponce's Landing to Doughty's Landing is essentially navy surplus. Long Island was the hub of naval activities in the bay, home to the US Navy Fuel Annex, Torpedo Control Officers School, and the US Naval Air Facility Casco Bay.

As Casco Bay Lines ferries approach Long Island, the two largest onshore structures are the great empty concrete hulk of the old navy boiler plant and the navy's former small boat maintenance facility, which now houses an auto repair shop, boat storage, and a variety store. The long, low buildings along Wharf Street, including Long Island Town Hall, were also left behind by the US Navy.

Just three miles long by one mile wide, Long Island was essentially partitioned during the war, with the navy commandeering the center section of the island for a fuel tank farm. Islanders and summer cottagers were relegated to the far ends of the island. Remnants of the island's past as a military reservation include not only the buildings along the waterfront, but also a dilapidated marine barracks, an unused guardhouse, a generator building, a litter of fences and fence posts running through the woods, and 15 empty underground fuel tanks.

Donald McVane, an island fisherman who still lives in the house where he was born 87 years ago, was a teenager when the war came to Long Island.

"We went from a quiet little summer resort island to crazy," recalls McVane. "It was the end of the Depression. The native islanders, with the exception of two or three lobstermen who were better off, were very poor. The war meant jobs."

But the war also meant that some islanders lost their homes. Sharon Doughty Marr was just an infant when her family came home one day to find a barricade erected in front of their home and an order to vacate the premises posted on the door. The navy was taking it by eminent domain.

"The war had a huge impact on a little place like this," says Marr. "Many families moved away because of it. We had people leave, but we also had navy people who stayed. We became friends with a lot of navy kids. The school was overloaded."

Marr recalls how the island fishermen all had large numbers painted on their boats so the military could readily identify them. Though some lobstermen set traps in among the anchored fleet, others chose to fish in the open ocean outside the sub nets.

Donald McVane inspects the former navy boiler plant on Long Island.
SCOTT SELL

Three of Marr's Doughty relatives from Chebeague are thought to be among the very few casualties of the war in Casco Bay. Captain Sidney Doughty and his sons Sidney Jr. and Roger set out one day in 1942 in their new fishing boat MARLENE and were never seen again.

"The story I always heard," says Marr, "was they may have had a run-in with a submarine. They never found anything."

In 1942, 8,245 Allied vessels were sunk in the Atlantic. Those numbers dropped precipitously the following year.

"Much of the reason for the 1943 turnaround during the Battle of the Atlantic," writes George Stewart in his history of naval operations on Casco Bay, "was the effectiveness of hunter-killer groups."

Hunter-killer groups consisted of destroyers and escort carriers that could launch planes to locate U-boats that the destroyers would then seek and destroy. Many of these ships set out to sea from Casco Bay.

"The hunter-killer groups were a vital part of winning the Battle of the Atlantic," says Stewart. "The U-boats had what they called their 'happy time' in the early 1940s when they ran wild along the East Coast. That all changed after we got all our ships out there."

Ship-aircraft operations helped to turn the tide of the war in the Atlantic. In the fall of 1942, the navy built a seaplane ramp and hangar at Doughty's Landing on Long Island.

"The fishermen on the island told them not to put the landing field there because of the prevailing winds," says Sharon Marr, "but the government didn't listen. The first plane that landed there crashed."

US Naval Air Facility Casco Bay, which for a short time was also used to launch drones as target practice for visiting ships, is now Johnson's Boatyard. The cement footprint of the hangar remains, and the in-ground tie-downs are used to secure boats rather than planes.

IN THE WAKE OF WAR

World War II departed Casco Bay as fast as it had arrived. Convoys of troops and their navy escorts fueled up and headed out across the North Atlantic for the 1944 D-Day landing. Just a year or so later, the hundreds of ships and thousands of military personnel and shipyard workers who contributed to the war effort began to drift away, and with them went the jobs that had pulled the country out of the Depression.

"When the war ended, nobody expected it," recalls Donald McVane. "Everyone was planning on another year or two of war because of Japan. Then we dropped the atomic bomb."

The advent of the atomic age—long-range bombers and nuclear missiles—rendered fixed harbor defense such as those rimming the shores of Casco Bay and the islands obsolete. The Coast Artillery was abolished in 1948, and the forts were disarmed and consigned to uncertain fates. Jewell Island, Two Lights, Fort Preble, Fort Gorges, Fort Williams, and portions of Peaks Island were acquired as public and park land. Fort McKinley on Great Diamond Island stood empty for 30 years before being redeveloped as an upscale resort community.

Out on Long Island, it took even longer to recover from war.

"One of the things you kept hearing at the beginning of

the war," says McVane, "was that after the war everybody would have a chance to buy back their property. That was pie in the sky."

In 1946, the Long Island Fuel Annex was designated an emergency fuel depot. There was a flurry of activity occasioned by the Cuban Missile Crisis in 1962, but that same year, the annex was placed on caretaker status. The US Navy kept a maintenance crew on the island until 1967, when the fuel annex was sold to King Resources as an oil tank farm. After a long and stormy history, the former military installation was sold to Northland Development, which placed some land in conservation and created a large-lot subdivision. But from 1942 until roughly 1996, Long Islanders were denied access to the heart of their island.

In 1957, a wildfire raced across Peaks Island, destroying all but a dozen of the military buildings. Battery Steele, the most prominent and important of the island's World War II relics, has served as a dumping ground, concert stage, and art venue. Over the years there have been proposals to convert the site into a mushroom farm, an international hotel and conference center, a wind farm, and an organic garden, but Battery Steele, maintained by the Peaks Island Land Preserve, remains undeveloped. And that's the way islanders want it.

"People out here don't want much more building," says former museum director Kimberly MacIsaac. "The resources can't take it."

On Long Island, Sharon Marr sees the island's military legacy as a mixed blessing. On the one hand, all the surplus buildings lend the island an air of faded glory; on the other, since Long Island declared its independence from Portland in 1993 and became a town, it has been able to make good use of some of the old navy buildings.

"The fire barn we have, the town hall, the recreation building, even the school, were put up by the government," says Marr. "Because of the underground oil tanks, the center of the island is a conservation area. It would be all house lots if we hadn't had the navy there."

"We made the best of a bad situation," agrees Donald McVane. "The land up there is filled with empty oil tanks, but it's a nice area now."

As World War II fades from living memory, the role that Casco Bay played in protecting the coast, providing the ships, hunting the subs, and mounting the invasion is easy to forget. But the islands remember. Landscapes punctuated by war surplus buildings and bunkers are a constant reminder that something historic happened there long ago.

"When you see how small we are," says Sharon Marr, "it's amazing the impact we had on that war." ♦

Edgar Allen Beem is a freelance writer who lives in Brunswick. He has been writing about the cultural life of Maine since 1978 for such publications as Maine Times, Down East, Yankee, Design New England *and* Island Journal. *He also writes a weekly column for the Greater Portland newspaper* The Forecaster.

Fort Gorges on Hog Island Ledge was used to store submarine mines during the war.
SCOTT SELL

JOEL WOODS

Fisherman // Photographer

My goal is not to make photography a career.

Very simply put, I am a fisherman, a working man who has learned to use a camera to capture the world as he sees it.

I have spent most of my life bobbing around the North Atlantic on massive steel boats, often for weeks on end. And as difficult and harsh as it is working on the sea, day in and day out, year-round, the men you work with can be just as hard.

It is not an environment that cultivates creativity. As a young man, hidden beneath my scowl, my bruised knuckles, my scars and tattoos, lay a powerful propensity toward the gentle and the artistic. But in those early years at sea, I wasn't in the least bit introspective. And even if I had been, even if I had wanted to create, when you're 150-odd miles offshore, where 24 hours on deck is not uncommon, having the time to create a ham sandwich is difficult; having the time to create something expressive is nearly impossible.

I had no idea when I purchased my first 35mm camera that it would be so instrumental—not only in my growth as a man, but in my growth as a human being. It would have been unfathomable for me to grasp at that time how this little machine could teach me patience. How it could teach me compassion. How it could teach me to see beauty in the smallest of things. How it could awaken in me something so powerful, something I didn't even know existed.

The speed at which I could create something is what made the camera a perfect vehicle for me. When we're on deck, we are always working. I didn't have the luxury of taking my time in order to get a shot. Once I saw a shot, I would remember it, but in order to capture it, I had to hone two very important skills.

First, I had to learn how to be quick. The moments worth capturing are often only there for a few seconds. I had to stop

what I was doing and run into the wheelhouse—sometimes having the time to take off my wet gloves, sometimes not (thus, the often-damaged equipment). I had to grab my camera out of the bag, often spilling its entire contents on the wheelhouse floor. I would then run back out on deck, trying to protect my camera as much as I could from the elements, quickly adjust the settings, focus it, frame the shot, and then capture it. I would then spin around, run back in the wheelhouse (scratching my head as I tried to remember where the heck I'd thrown my lens cover), stow the camera back in the bag, and run back out on deck to promptly get back to work.

Second, I had to learn how to see the future—abstractly, anyway. I had to recognize when something was going to happen before it actually did. Sometimes when I see a shot while working, I know it will be months before the conditions are exactly the same and I get a chance to capture it again.

I think this quickness and haste can be seen in my images. I can see it in the hyper-fast shutter speed that captures all the motion with such clarity—how every drop of seawater is frozen in place. But I can also see it in the flaws—how I didn't get the chance to adjust the setting quite the way I wanted to. Maybe the image is a little out of focus. Maybe it's a bit grainy, perhaps not framed well. Sometimes I can't use the image at all.

Unfortunately, this is a by-product of shooting in such conditions. And I gladly accept all of it. Even if I never had the opportunity to take a single image, I am grateful that I've had the chance to see this beauty daily.

For there will come a time when I am too old to spend my days on the water. Instead, I will be sitting quietly, thinking of years past, lucky to have my images to bring me back, recalling each of these days at sea as a gift.

I do not take credit for anything I capture. I am just fortunate to work in such an amazing and beautiful environment. Though she can be quite moody, the sea is an easy subject to photograph. ♦

Joel Woods lives in the Midcoast region of Maine, and is on the deck of a lobster boat nine months out of the year around Matinicus Island. He spends the remainder of the year fishing out of New Bedford, Massachusetts. He is active in the lawmaking and regulatory process in Maine and is currently fighting for fishermen's rights. Together with his fellow fishermen, he is an active and proud member of the Maine Lobstering Union, an associate organization of The International Association of Machinists and Aerospace Workers (IAMAW). He is eternally grateful for the sacrifices our servicemen and women have made for all of us. Thus, the lion's share of income generated from his photographs have gone directly to charity. Pam Payeur of the Wounded Heroes Program of Maine and Mike Jackson of Grundens USA have been particularly supportive in directing some of these proceeds and goods to disabled veterans.

A Community Unraveled
The Legacy of Ireland's Great Blasket Island

STORY AND PHOTOS BY KATHLEEN WALSH BUCHANAN

The Dingle Peninsula in County Kerry, Ireland, is a landscape of spare and emotive beauty. It is a rugged place of stone-walled fields climbing mountainsides to the limits of tillable land, where the Atlantic Ocean meets bold headlands with an almost unimaginable energy and intensity.

Irish poet and philosopher John O'Donohue's words describe this corner of Ireland well: "There is a curvature of the landscape, a color and shape that constantly frustrate the eye anxious for symmetry or linear simplicity."

Three miles off the western end of the Dingle Peninsula lies an archipelago of islands called the Blasket Islands. They are at the far edge of Ireland, with the great pyramid

peak of the island Tearacht forming the most westerly point in the country. The largest of the islands, the Great Blasket, gracefully curves upward from the Atlantic with skyline contours unobstructed by trees or structures. It is approximately three miles long on its east-west axis and a half-mile wide from north to south, rising to an elevation of almost 1,000 feet above the ocean.

Facing the mainland to the east and sheltered in the gently curving bowl of the mountainside lies an abandoned village that once sheltered a community of fishermen, farmers, and their families.

At its peak population in 1911, the village was home to approximately 160 people. In the years after World War I, emigration of the island's youth, the decline of the fishing industry, and insufficient communication and transport to the mainland created vulnerability for the small community. The number of residents steadily declined, resulting in a largely aging population exposed to the extreme conditions on the island. Driven by increasing hardships and struggling to survive, in the late 1940s the islanders began to lobby the government to be relocated to homes on the mainland.

The eventual evacuation finally came in 1953, hastened by a tragic death. But the islanders' story continued, with another chapter written in western Massachusetts.

Today, all that remains are the drystone walls of village homes and fields in various degrees of decay, and the roads and pathways that speak to the rhythms of a community and way of life that has disappeared from this beautiful place.

I first visited the Great Blasket Island in 2000 and was instantly captivated by the landscape. It was a point of transition in my life, having just made the decision to leave my job as a wildlife biologist to pursue an art career full-time, and I was using my time in Ireland to plan my path forward. With that goal guiding me, I found myself

seeking quiet places, the edges and open spaces.

I visited the Great Blasket for a day, hopping on a ferry from the village of Dunquin over to the small landing on the island. I recall climbing the hill above the village, sketchbook in hand, marveling at the lines of the landscape—all rolling curves and vertiginous angles falling to the hard horizontal of the Atlantic horizon.

It is an island of unusual, almost surreal beauty. The complete lack of flat ground gives one a sense of being perpetually perched above the water, with the ground rolling away to the sea under your feet. Sheep belonging to mainland farmers graze the island, keeping the vegetation cropped close to the soil. Wild rabbits are so abundant that as you walk the hillsides, handfuls scatter from your path into burrows and under stones.

In the years since the village has been inhabited, significant colonies of shearwaters, auks, fulmars, and Atlantic gray seals have made the island their home. I left at the end of the day with a very fragmented sensory experience: the yielding softness of the turf underfoot, the sound of the wind roaring through a fulmar's wings as it banked around me near the island summit, the shift of light and cloud, and the pure blue-green of the Atlantic. I left determined to spend time making artwork about the island, to integrate the patchwork of a day's experience into a more meaningful whole.

~

The story of the Great Blasket and its community is one that is woven tightly into the Irish language. The Dingle Peninsula is part of the Gaeltacht, a region where Irish is recognized as the predominant language. Because of its relative isolation, the Irish spoken on the Great Blasket was a pure form of the language, uncorrupted by the English spoken throughout much of mainland Ireland.

In the early 20th century, this attracted linguistic scholars from throughout Europe to the island to study the language, and who in turn encouraged the islanders to record their way of life in writing. The result was the emergence of literary talent that captured the intimate structure of the community, the rhythm and cadence of conversation, and the cooperative nature of both work and social traditions.

Three islanders stand apart for their contribution to the island literature: Tomás O'Crohan (*The Islandman, Island Cross-Talk*), Maurice O'Sullivan (*Twenty Years A-Growing*), and Peig Sayers (*Peig,* and *An Old Woman's Reflections*). Each is a unique voice, with individual perspectives on island life born from differences in age, gender, and experience. All three were gifted storytellers, with remarkable eyes for detail. What emerges are lyrical accounts of daily work on sea and land, the natural kinship of the islanders born of necessity and isolation, and both the joys and hardships of living on this exposed, wild island.

In *The Islandman*, published in 1934, O'Crohan writes with a keen awareness that the way of life of the Great Blasket community was

slipping away: "I have written minutely of much that we did, for it was my wish that somewhere there should be a memorial of it all, and I have done my best to set down the character of the people about me so that some record of us might live after us, for the like of us will never be again."

In effect, this became the island's epitaph.

Four years after my first visit, I had the opportunity to return to the Great Blasket for an extended stay. Funded by a travel grant from the Connecticut-based Amity Art Foundation, the plan was to draw and photograph the island for a month and then return home to create a finished body of art from the field work. (As a printmaker, my work requires the use of a large etching press, and thus can't be done outside.)

Arriving unceremoniously off the ferry from Dingle in driving wind and rain, my husband and I quickly created a home base within the remains of a village home, pitching our tent within the windbreak of the drystone walls. We adjusted quickly to the rhythm of life on the Great Blasket—rising early with the light, spending days hiking to the far reaches of the island, drawing sheep, seabirds, seals, and the landscape whenever the absence of rain allowed. We would lie on the turf at the tops of sea cliffs watching gannets, basking sharks, porpoises, auks. Everywhere there was color, light, and life to be recorded.

Evenings were centered on cooking a hot meal on the backpacking stove, making tea, and immersing ourselves in the voices of the island writers by the light of our headlamps. For me, it was an incredibly emotional experience to be walking the landscape and standing within the walls of homes where the island literature is rooted. It is unsettling to have the past and present intersect in such an incongruous way—to be immersed in a landscape that speaks of absence and a community unraveled, and yet to have the voices of the villagers present all around you. It is like standing quietly in the presence of souls.

Every night, after sleeping for a few hours, we would be awakened around midnight by the cries of Manx shearwaters returning to their colony on the island. It is a difficult sound to describe—not at all bird-like, but rather a raspy, wheezing, mournful wail. We would crawl out of our sleeping bags into the wind and point our headlamps into the blackness above, hoping to catch a glimpse of the elusive seabirds that sounded as though they were circling just above our heads. We were never able to see them; their voices were all we had.

I left the island at the end of the month with sketchbooks and head full, and spent the next two years creating 25 editions of collagraph prints from my time there. The work was exhibited throughout New England and New York, and I still feel great fondness for the project that helped me establish my printmaking career. In the course of exhibiting the work, I was always surprised by the number of people I met who either have a personal or family connection to the Great Blasket, or who feel a kinship through the island literature. It is a place that is truly beloved by many.

≈

Perhaps no one personifies this dedication to the Great Blasket more than Dr. Michael Carney. In the early 20th century, a dozen or so islanders emigrated to my hometown of Springfield, Massachusetts, following each other's path toward economic opportunity, and seeking to plant

Michael Carney at his home in East Longmeadow, Massachusetts

Island boys stand for a photo on the beach called "An Trá Bán," which translates from Irish to "The White Strand." Michael Carney is standing in the back on the left, and three of his brothers—Tom, Martin, and Paddy—are sitting in front.
COURTESY OF OPW GREAT BLASKET CENTRE

roots in America near family and familiar faces from the island. Michael was part of this tradition, leaving the island in 1937 in search of work and social opportunity.

He spent his childhood and early teen years on the island, eventually moving to Cahersiveen briefly, then Dublin, and in 1948, to the United States, settling in Springfield. Three of his father's brothers had emigrated from the island to Springfield in the 1920s, thus giving him social and family support upon his arrival. His memoir, *From the Great Blasket to America*, was published in 2013, adding the emigrant perspective to the canon of island literature.

I sat down with him in December 2014 at his home, with Raidió na Gaeltachta (Irish language public radio) playing quietly in the background. The walls of his living room were decorated with photos and paintings of the

Great Blasket, and I was welcomed warmly to sit beside him and talk about the island.

At 94, Michael has lived the majority of his life in America, but his voice still holds the soft accent of a native Irish speaker. We thumbed through my photographs of the island, letting the familiar landmarks of his childhood home spark stories of island life. He is quick with his humor, and a vivid storyteller whose absolute dedication to the Great Blasket is quickly apparent.

He spoke to me about the unique character of the community where he was raised.

"As children, you had to create your own pastimes. We would snare rabbits to eat, setting the snares on their runways. We would collect gull eggs from Beginish. You had to watch your head as you collected them, with the gulls swooping down at you. You played football on the strand—our ball was made of old socks stuffed with grass. There was tug-of-war, dancing, storytelling . . .

"[Islanders] never complained about helping each other. You became one family, because otherwise you had no reason to be there. My father had a flock of seventy to eighty sheep, and we would farm potatoes, cabbage, and turnip. If someone ran short we would share. When you had to borrow something like milk, tea, or sugar when you ran short, the first thing you would do is return it when you got more. You never owed anyone anything."

In the wake of World War II, opportunities for emigration and employment off the Great Blasket were abundant. With the island's youth emigrating, insecurity in fishing, and the closure of the island school, the community structure had become extremely vulnerable. Young people from the mainland were reluctant to marry into

island families, as the conditions were so challenging and the island's future seemed so uncertain. Few young people remained, and those who did struggled to find a way to support themselves on the island.

The winter of 1946–47 brought some of the harshest conditions that the islanders had seen in recent years. Their only transportation to and from the island was the traditional *naomhóg*, a small canvas-on-frame rowing vessel, and the only way to communicate with the mainland was a single battery-operated telephone with unreliable service. The rough weather resulted in complete isolation.

In December of 1946, Michael's younger brother Seán fell ill. Unable to

communicate with the mainland or reach a doctor due to the rough seas, Seán died on January 9, 1947, of meningitis. He was 24 years old. The prolonged tragedy of the young man's death proved to be a pivotal point for the community.

In his memoir, Michael writes, "It all seemed so senseless. The islanders came to the conclusion that it was no place for them to live. Essentially, Seán's death and the circumstances broke the will of the islanders to continue living on the island. It was time to move on."

From his home in Dublin, Michael played a major role in lobbying the Irish government to help relocate the remaining islanders to the mainland, writing to the Taoiseach (Prime Minister of Ireland) Éamon de Valera about Seán's death and the hardships facing the community, and asking for property on the mainland to relocate the remaining islanders.

He also approached members of the Irish Parliament, exerting pressure to get aid for the islanders. De Valera visited the island in July 1947 to see the conditions for himself, but did not act before being ousted from office in 1948. This resulted in six years of frustration for the islanders, with the new Taoiseach, John Costello, not moving on behalf of the community. De Valera came back into office in 1951, and the government soon decided that all remaining islanders were to be moved to the mainland.

That came in 1953, with just 22 people living on the island. They were given homes and land in Dunquin, where they could fish and farm within view of the Great Blasket. Although islanders continued to raise sheep and spend some weeks of the summer on the island, the Great Blasket was essentially abandoned after the evacuation, the village left to the elements and the island to the seabirds and seals.

In the 1970s, property began to be purchased from former island families by an American developer with plans to create a resort on the Great Blasket. The plan eventually fell through, and in 1985 Michael learned that the Great Blasket was being advertised for sale in the *Wall Street Journal* for $900,000.

"Well, that's when I started to get my Irish up," he recalled. "I said, 'Over my dead body.'"

The reaction in Ireland was similar, with many shocked at the potential private sale of a place that held such cultural significance.

West Kerry locals worked to establish the non-profit Blasket Island Foundation in 1987, with a mission to keep the spirit and memory of the island alive. From Springfield, Michael and the Blasket community supported this objective with fundraising efforts. The group funded a study on the creation of the Blasket Centre in Dunquin, which paved the way for the government to invest in the project. The Blasket Centre was built in 1993, and serves an important role in preserving the island legacy, drawing over 40,000 visitors each year.

The Blasket Island Foundation also has promoted efforts to preserve the island and, eventually, to create the Great Blasket Island National Historic Park. Michael has played a role in the process, meeting with members of the US Congress and two Irish presidents to promote preservation of the Great Blasket.

Moving the island from private to state ownership has been a slow and complex process. Presently, approximately 70 percent of the island is in government hands, and while the island is not yet officially a national park, Michael is hopeful that that day will come soon.

"There are only nine of us left—six in Ireland and three in Springfield," he said, referring to the remaining native islanders. "When we all expire, I hope the government has taken over complete occupation of the island. Then I will sleep better.

"I feel the island has given so much. I would like the memory of the people there to not be forgotten," he told me.

He paused, and quietly said, "I feel the island deserves this." ♦

Kathleen Walsh Buchanan lives in Thomaston with her husband and two children. Her printmaking studio, Grey Seal Press, is named after the seal colony on Great Blasket Island. She will be returning to Ireland this fall for a residency fellowship at the Ballinglen Art Foundation, in Ballycastle, County Mayo.

*The author sketching on a hill
near the western end of the island*

Research sources:
From the Great Blasket to America, Michael Carney with Gerald Hayes (Collins Press, 2014)
The Islandman, Tomás O'Crohan (Talbot Press, 1934)
Anam Cara, John O'Donohue (HarperCollins, 1997)
The Blasket Islands: Next Parish America, Ray Stagles and Joan Stagles (O'Brien Press, 1998)

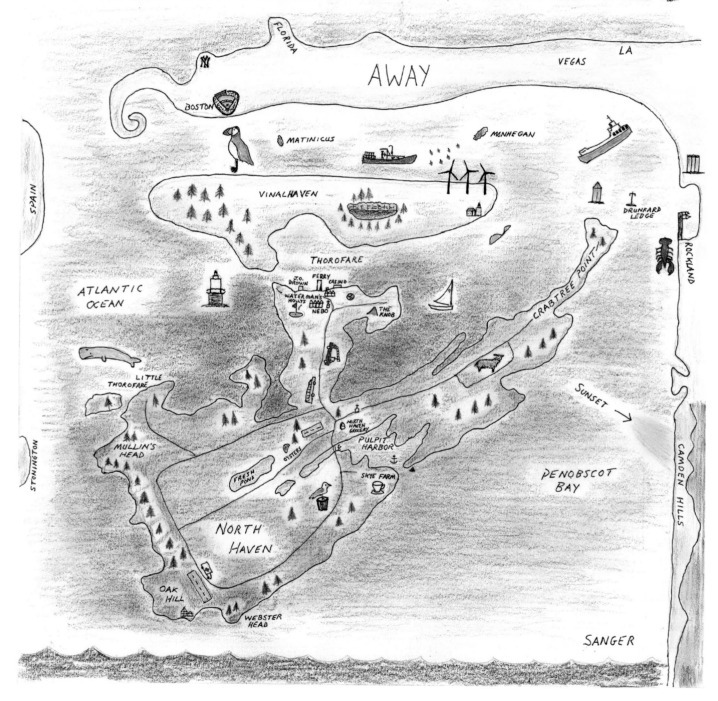

Alex Sanger, a longtime seasonal resident of North Haven, created a map of the island as a humorous send-up of Saul Steinberg's illustration, *View of the World from 9th Avenue* which served as the March 29, 1976, cover of the *New Yorker*. Like Steinberg's Manhattan, Sanger sees North Haven as the center of the world. ♦

Stonington: A Town on the Edge

Contradictions abound, but resiliency abides

STORY AND PHOTOS BY TOM GROENING

If anyone has a finger on the pulse of a community, it's the guy who runs the town's weekly newspaper. And what does Ben Barrows, general manager of the *Island Ad-Vantages,* think about his hometown?

"On any given day, I might feel discouraged or hopeful," he admits. "Everything we need to be successful is here—human creativity and resourcefulness."

But others worry that such success could mean Stonington loses its genuine quality, a feature valued by newcomers and natives alike. That could mean someone like Kathleen Billings-Pezaris, the native-born town manager, might not be able to afford a home in Stonington.

Still others, like longtime fishermen Frank Gotwals and Jeff Dworsky, both of whom arrived in the early 1970s, say forces already have wrought significant change in Stonington. Yet Robin Alden, who heads up a nonprofit working to support local fishing, says even bigger changes may be on the horizon if lobster populations suddenly crash.

The forces and features that define Stonington seem contradictory. But in conversation with some who have witnessed the town's last chapter being written, and those who are writing its next, those contradictions tell the story.

~

By boat, Stonington is a short hop east from the Fox Islands Thoroughfare. From the tourist-choked streets of Rockland, it is less than 20 miles away, as the crow flies. But in other, consequential ways, Stonington is a world away, a town very much on the edge of an island, and on the edge of a way of life.

It's on an island, at the southern tip of Deer Isle, yet that island is connected to the mainland by a bridge. The bridge allows lobster—20 million pounds or more each year, perennially making it the top lobster-landing port in the state—to be carried by truck to market.

But Stonington is isolated. For most of Maine's residents and tourists, it's easier to get to Vinalhaven. Locals are quick to point out that it's an hour's drive from US Route 1, and, of course, another hour and more from I-95.

There are more contradictions.

Stonington's downtown has the gritty quality you would expect in a fishing town. A notice posted in the town office hints at the rough-around-the-edges life, scolding fishermen for "unnecessary tire noise, driving to endanger, breaking of bottles, vulgar language, etc." at the pier.

"Everything we need to be successful is here: human creativity and resourcefulness."
—*Ben Barrows*

Such bad behavior probably is confined to the hours after dark, when day-trippers are long gone and other visitors have retired to their rooms in the motel or in the inns. Just in case those visitors missed the in-plain-sight evidence, signs on trash cans remind them that Stonington is a working waterfront community.

The tourists do come, though, because the town is chock-full of attractive homes and commercial buildings, tucked into a hillside that gives long views down Penobscot Bay, and of scores of working lobster boats. It's an alluring place that has brought artists summer after summer, and the number of galleries in the tiny downtown suggests they are able to sell their work.

These contradictions have been at work for decades and are part of its strength, say Stonington's key players. But they worry about its future. The largest contrary forces, it seems, are the inevitable changes that will roll down the peninsula and onto Deer Isle, and the deep desire of many for Stonington to remain an authentic fishing town.

≈

The *Island Ad-Vantages* newspaper office where Ben Barrows meets with me has a spare, old-fashioned look. The building could serve as a set for an early-20th-century period film. Some of the look is by design; Barrows, 33, general manager of the company that runs the Stonington weekly, as well as the *Castine Patriot* and the (Blue Hill) *Weekly Packet*, has a manual typewriter and an early Apple computer on shelves over his desk.

His father, Nat Barrows, has owned the papers for the past 30-plus years. Ben has returned to the town in which he grew up and attended high school to help out his father, but not before seeing a bit of the world. Actually, he's seen a lot of the world—Antarctica, Iraq, Jordan, Afghanistan, various African countries—all in humanitarian service.

While pride in Stonington is evident, he is frank about its shortcomings, as seen through the eyes of a young man: "The lack of access to ethnic food, other cultures and their ideas." But returning after a dozen years traveling the world, Barrows embraces "the opportunity to have depth rather than breadth."

He serves as a town selectman, a post he takes seriously.

Stonington has changed in the years he's been away, with "more people, more development," but "the essential aspects of its identity are unchanged," he said.

Change is inevitable, though.

"Eventually, those outside forces will make their way into this community."

We talk about fishing and tourism, trophy homes and trailers, and he is thoughtful, analytical, but very much leaning into the work of keeping the town vital.

The town has a sense of place, "and a fierce pride in what we do. The fact that we're off the beaten path—the end of the road, literally—makes it a special place. There's a bounty of blessings from the natural world," he says, meaning everything from lobster to the cool sea breezes of summer.

But when that inevitable change does come, "It's not going to be a smooth trajectory."

History provides some hope, though.

"We started as a granite town, and then we were a shipbuilding town, and then a fishing town," and it wasn't lobster, but cod that filled the holds and paid the bills. "All of those things have collapsed, yet the town has carried on. It's still a great place to live and work. We're tough."

In the context of our hour-plus conversation, that's not a trite, ready-made chamber of commerce quote. Barrows speaks authoritatively of the struggle to adapt, to remain vital and authentic.

"Questions of identity are never really far behind balancing the working waterfront and cruisers and tourism," he says, then pauses. "Sometimes I feel we have to sort out the identity thing first."

≈

Frank Gotwals moved to Stonington in 1973, taking a leave of absence from college. His family had ties to the island, and he summered here as a child. His first work came in raking sea moss, then, in 1976, he began lobstering.

"That led to one thing after another, and I never left."

Landing at one of the three buying stations on a perfect late September afternoon, Gotwals's boat, SEA SONG, stands out. It's remarkably clean, a two-year-old wooden boat. He and his sternman, a young woman, efficiently sort their catch, then he grabs a cup of coffee from the store and we talk, sitting in the shade of the statue of a granite cutter.

Blond and handsome, he looks younger than his 59 years, despite being on the water all day. That look suits the other life he's had, playing guitar and singing his own songs. He's put out CDs, including *Beach Glass* and *Unfamiliar Sea* (both available on iTunes), and the music is solid singer-songwriter fare, flavored by references to his fishing life, boosted by his exceptional finger-picking guitar work.

Though he no longer tours through New England, he still plays out, often performing with others.

In the early 1970s, he would have stood out as a summer person doing something unusual, trying to make Stonington his home. Back then, "most of the downtown houses were local families," Gotwals says.

Until the early 1980s, there were two grocery stores, a hardware store, a pharmacy, and other businesses that made the town more self-sufficient. "There was one real estate agent when I was a kid," he remembers, "and then all of a sudden, there were five or six," he says, letting that fact explain larger forces at work.

He's not bitter, not nostalgic exactly, but more philosophical about the changes. Or maybe just tired from a long week of fishing.

Everyone in a fishing town like Stonington has thought about the unthinkable—a collapse of lobstering.

"It's always been unpredictable," Gotwals says. "But there's no other options, as far as fishing. If we don't have lobstering, we won't be a fishing town, and we will have to reinvent ourselves. I also know I made a living at it, in some really lean times," he adds, suggesting that being prudent about saving and investing is key.

The fishing pier saw state and federal investment in the late 1980s and early 1990s, Gotwals recalled, after the United States asserted its rights over near-shore fishing, kicking out fish-factory ships from Russia and other nations. "At the time, there were a fair amount of gill-net boats out of Stonington," he said. But that fishery did not rebound as expected.

The summer renters and second-home buyers have given the village a prosperous sheen, but that doesn't tell the whole story.

"There's a lot of people here who struggle," Gotwals says. Land costs have gone up. The young woman who works on his boat lives on the other side of the bridge, as do many in her economic situation.

Forty years after leaving college for Stonington, he's got no regrets.

"This always seemed like home to me. I like living here—I like what it has to offer. I've been fortunate to make an interesting life here. I choose to live here," he says, and with a grin, adds, "I'm still on my leave of absence from college."

～

Like Gotwals, Jeff Dworsky also arrived in Stonington in 1973. A photographer by trade (his excellent documentary

Jeff Dworsky

48

Unloading the day's catch at one of Stonington's lobster co-ops

work was featured in *Island Journal* in the mid-1990s), Dworsky began lobstering in those early years.

At that time, 95 percent of the homes were owned by fishermen.

"There were all these beautiful homes and shorefront," he says, pointing out a favorite bought by a seasonal resident a few years ago.

Dworsky, 59, came to town from Cambridge, Massachusetts, but he expresses a native's curmudgeonly crankiness about changes—a description he chuckles at when I make it—that have unfurled over the decades.

"I was the beginning of the wave," he admits, as he and others of his generation left cities for rural Maine. At just 17, he and three others split the rent on a building that previously "had been a whorehouse," he says.

Today, the seasonal and second-home residents complain about drunk fishermen and locals driving too fast, he claims, trying to neuter what he sees as "the rugged independence" of the place. "But it was also gentle and kind and giving," and neighbors were nice to each other. Today, "They're not getting along. All those fences went up," he says.

"When I first came here, this was too far from the major cities to be attractive for seasonal homes," he says.

That's changed.

One seasonal resident whom Dworsky counts as a friend is Jill Hoy. Hoy, 60, paints lovely realistic landscapes and runs a gallery in town. She's been summering here since she was nine. Artists, like fishermen, struggle to make it in Stonington, she says. And the arts have been good for the economy, she believes.

"People follow artists, oftentimes, and they often follow beauty," Hoy says. "I see a lot of Swedish and German travelers, and I ask them how they came to visit." They tell her they looked at a map, saw the town at the end of the peninsula, and were intrigued enough to visit.

"We're lucky to be as far down Route 15 as we are," she says. "It preserves it, to some extent. It immediately rules out a lot of people," who don't make the effort to visit.

~

Few have had both the longevity and insider status to understand Stonington as well as Kathleen Billings-Pezaris, the town manager. Growing up in the 1960s and '70s, and graduating from the high school in 1981, she's as native as they come.

There's no hesitation as she describes the town of her childhood: "Poor."

But waves of building came in the subsequent decades. Is a tipping point coming?

"Yeah, I worry about that," she says. Many more people are "buying across the Reach," on the mainland side of the bridge. "Housing is going to be a problem. When is it that I can't afford to live on the island?"

Half of the water company's customers shut off their service in the winter, an indication of how seasonal the downtown has become. But the newcomers and the arts have injected money and energy.

"I think it's a positive—the more that we can diversify, as a community and an economy, the better off we are," says Billings-Pezaris, although she admits she sometimes hears locals say there are too many galleries in town.

Another source of energy and investment came from wealthy financier Donald Sussman, who once owned a nearby summer residence, she says. He bought and renovated large waterfront and Main Street buildings, one of which became the improved grocery store, and the other, home to Penobscot East Resource Center, a nonprofit that works to support fishing.

"We were lucky someone was willing to invest in some of these properties," Billings-Pezaris says. The improvements spurred others to fix up their homes and businesses, she believes.

As manager, her goals are to see a vibrant, fishing harbor, stronger shoulder seasons for tourism, and for the town's authenticity to remain intact.

~

Fishing dominates Stonington's economy. Or, maybe better put, Stonington dominates fishing. It's Maine's top lobster-landing port, year after year. In 2013, more than 20 million pounds were landed, at a value of $43 million. There are 300 to 400 independently owned fishing boats in the harbor. Nationally, the port ranks 21st for value of catch and 43rd by volume.

Fishing is what brought Robin Alden to Stonington, but not to haul traps or set nets. Alden, who, like Dworsky, hails from Cambridge, Massachusetts, took a year off from Yale University in 1971 and stayed on the island, later finishing her degree at the University of Maine. In 1973 she founded *Commercial Fisheries News,* which she operated for 20 years. Other than the three years she served as marine resources commissioner under Governor Angus King, Alden never left town.

Now the director of Penobscot East Resource Center, the nonprofit that works to ensure that locals can "fish forever," as its motto puts it, she has seen the changes and challenges Stonington has faced, but remains optimistic about the future.

"The downtown has changed dramatically," Alden says. When she arrived, it was a bustling and self-contained year-round community. Now, in winter, "It's pretty close to a ghost town," she says.

"Some of the changes in the culture of the town, the activities of the town, have come from the retirees," Alden notes. Many retirees have been active in the community, and Alden sees that as a positive. "I like the mix of people who live here."

Asked about a possible collapse of the lobster industry, she redirects the question.

"I think we should look at the strengths." Each of the harbor's fishing boats represents an independently owned business, she says, and each creates ripples in the local economy.

Alden knows the record lobster catches of recent years are not likely to last, given that they exceed—by about fivefold—the long-term averages.

"We're in some kind of ecological bubble," she says. "What we don't know is how gracefully the industry will contract if the resource contracts."

But there is much to be optimistic about, Alden believes.

"We ship out an incredible amount of granite," she notes, a resurgence in an industry that was dominant in the 19th century. Billings Shipyard is thriving, serving the many working and pleasure boats that pass through the area.

~

Linda Nelson is recommended to me again and again as a must-interview source. Early in 2015, Nelson was appointed assistant director of the state's arts commission, and so will be working in Augusta. It's a job she's earned, most Stonington residents would agree.

Like many Maine coastal towns (Belfast, Camden, Rockport, Boothbay), Stonington has an opera house, the result of a much earlier generation's ideas of bringing culture to the rugged coast. But here, it's more than a pretty old building; it's been the nursery for a vibrant arts scene.

That's because Nelson and three other women arrived in town in 1999 and set out to revive the local arts, a tradition that extends back to the 1890s, when the opera house was built. It burned in 1910, but a new one was built in 1912.

A nonprofit—Opera House Arts—was established in 1999 to both restore the building, which had sat vacant for eight years, and to provide a variety of arts programming for the community.

Nelson recalls meeting with town selectmen who "wholeheartedly supported" the plan. Did the community embrace or resist the vision?

"A combination of those things," she remembers, in part because four women—"four gay women," she wryly notes—were the driving force. The town seemed to take a wait-and-see approach, she says, but when the women proved they could work hard to achieve their goals, people got on board.

Nelson hails from Stonington, Connecticut, and coming to Maine's Stonington was by design. A Bowdoin grad, she knew Maine, and Stonington.

"It's a great place. I think it's one of the last genuine places," she says. "We wanted to be part of a real working community. Stonington is one of a very few communities with an extractive industry"—lobstering—"which is thriving. We wanted to create culture that has real meaning" for people of such a community, she says.

The opera house features films, staged readings, plays, live music, and other performances, and the organization offers arts programs in the local schools. It generates at least $1 million in economic activity in the area, Nelson believes.

"We're always working to create diversity. We have to promote Stonington as a destination," she says, with the arts offerings part of that effort.

Will Stonington retain its genuineness, the quality that drew her?

"I think it will, because people want that."

∾

Fishing brought Brent Oliver, 54, back to Stonington and his family's roots. His father, a native, had followed fish to other ports, but returned here with his family in 1969.

By 1983, the younger Oliver was working in gill netting, but federal regulations seemed to thwart his efforts. From 1996 on, he has been lobstering full-time.

As important as fishing has been to him, Oliver sees a bigger-picture future for the town.

"It will stay a fishing town," he says, "but we need more than just fishermen on this island. If we could have six months of July and August [tourist activity], it would thrive. I welcome the tourists, as long as they don't want to change the world."

In the 1990s, Oliver saw retirees move to the area and run for school board and selectmen seats, a trend he believes was not good for the town. Yet change must come, he says, and he welcomes technological and commercial advances.

"The world is changing, and I don't want to see Deer Isle and Stonington left behind." ♦

Tom Groening is editor of Island Journal *and* The Working Waterfront.

The campers and staff of the Vinalhaven Friends Junior Work Camp ALL PHOTOS AND ILLUSTRATIONS COURTESY OF THE AFSC ARCHIVES

The Summer of '43, When Quakers Landed on Vinalhaven

While World War II raged, urban teens visited a Maine island to work

BY HARRY GRATWICK

By 1943, the World War seemed endless. The news carried stories of victories and defeats, liberation and slaughter.

In February of that year, the German siege of Stalingrad in Russia ended, but in Poland, the Warsaw Ghetto had been destroyed. In May, Germany's Afrika Korps surrendered. This was followed by the devastation of Hamburg, the result of Allied bombing, in July. In the Pacific, after eight bloody months, the Guadalcanal campaign was successful, and in August, the young John Kennedy's PT boat was sunk in the Solomon Islands.

But for a group of high school students at a Quaker work camp on the Penobscot Bay island of Vinalhaven, the war must have seemed far away. Recently, logs dutifully recorded by campers and staff during that summer were discovered in the archives of the American Friends Service Committee (AFSC) in Philadelphia. They provide a glimpse of that island experience over seventy years ago.

The Quaker commitment to peace would be recognized only after the horrors of that worldwide conflict. The organization won the Nobel Peace Prize in 1946 and 1947.

The previous August, Edward R. Miller, representing AFSC, had visited Vinalhaven seeking a site for a Quaker work camp. In his report, Miller bluntly described a town that had fallen on hard times. What had been a flourishing boatbuilding, shipping, quarrying, and fishing community had declined to the extent that mainland banks were refusing loans to anyone on the island.

Miller's views may seem a harsh evaluation for someone who had only visited Vinalhaven for a few days. Although there was still some lobstering and a couple of dairy farms, people were leaving the island in droves to look for jobs on the mainland, and many of the young men had enlisted in the military. An additional problem was that the island ferry had been pressed into service by the US Coast Guard.

URBAN TEENS

The 20 teenagers in the work camp were a varied lot: most were from Philadelphia, New York, and Boston, although several were refugees from Europe. The group arrived in Rockland by train and was transported to Vinalhaven by lobster boat. Arriving after dark, they trudged up a hill to an old house—which locals said was haunted—with no electricity above the first floor. Things looked better in the daylight, and the first weekend was spent settling in and repairing what would be their home for the next two months.

Bill Carey and Karl Spaeth are now in their 80s, but both remember that summer. Carey, who teaches pediatric medicine at Children's Hospital in Philadelphia, recalls spending most of his time working on the town hall, the building now occupied by the Vinalhaven Historical Society.

"We lived in a house about fifty yards away. The girls, and a chaperone, were on the second floor; the boys were on the

Drawings and inside jokes
from the work camp log

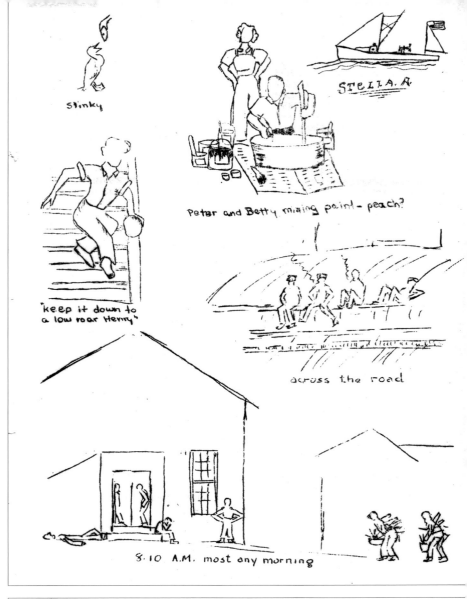

third. The first floor was used for Quaker meetings and recreation, such as record playing. There was running water but the toilets were indoor privies," he recalled recently. The group leaders and the cook stayed in an adjacent house.

"The purpose of the work camp," Carey explained, "besides keeping a group of generally overprivileged adolescents busy, was to bring some amateur construction to aid a rather poor seacoast town. I got used to sustained physical work as never before. Our chief recreation was swimming in the quarry. A great treat was to go down to the drugstore for a Boston Cooler, a delicious mixture of root beer and vanilla ice cream."

Spaeth is a retired lawyer, and today remembers being the youngest member of the group. He had just finished eighth grade at Germantown Friends School, and was nicknamed "the professor" by some of the older students, who were impressed with his knowledge of the sciences, well developed for someone not yet in high school.

Our campers are more chummy than ever with various local boys. Dreamy, Herbert Junior, Penny, Ralph, Weepy, Victor, and the rest are personalities we shan't forget.

—from the camp log

The major project, repair of the town hall, began almost immediately. "We joyously and noisily tore down the lockers with menacing-looking wrecking bars," Spaeth remembers.

For the rest of the summer, campers were scattered around the building, removing interior partitions, excess lumber, and trash. Then it was on to plastering, putting up drywall, replacing windows, and, finally, painting the walls and ceiling. Rebuilding the stage, reinforcing the balcony, and constructing two dressing rooms were particularly challenging jobs, the men remember.

Spaeth also remembers the campers spending considerable time digging an extensive drainage ditch around a nearby schoolhouse. That project provided a practical upgrade, because in previous winters, children had had to wade through water to get into the building. Loads of granite chips were lugged in to fill up the ditch,

which was then covered with sand.

On the playground, new sandboxes with covers were built, and new swing sets, slides, and a seesaw were installed. Finally, the entire area was leveled and resurfaced with gravel.

COMMUNITY INTERACTION

The staff was concerned that the work camp not be seen as a summer frolic by a bunch of rich kids from East Coast prep schools. As a result, every effort was made to follow through on work projects while engaging the Vinalhaven community on a variety of levels.

Over time, integration with the community succeeded. Twice a week "Play Day" programs were established for younger island children, and the staff was gratified when as many as forty children would show up. At the end of the summer, there was an enthusiastic and well-attended grand opening of the town hall, complete with skits, songs, and a recital by the camp band.

The local teens were a hard sell, though. In the log, a counselor recorded his observations: "The day usually began with a gallery of local boys lounging on the fence across the road. . . . [They were] cigarette-smoking, ice-cream-eating lads with a high incidence of profanity."

As the summer progressed, though, the logs noted that the attitudes toward the visitors changed: "We had a good deal of help from village youths. Yesterday there were six of them helping out."

Of course, the town selectmen added leverage, repeatedly urging island boys and girls to pitch in on the projects.

As the Vinalhaven boys began hanging around with increasing frequency, the camp log reported: "Our campers are more chummy than ever with various local boys. They are no longer problem youths to us. Dreamy, Herbert Junior, Penny, Ralph, Weepy, Victor, and the rest are personalities we shan't forget."

At the end of the workday, there were always a few island boys wanting to know if anyone (especially the girls) wanted to go swimming. In fact, on many afternoons, most of the campers went swimming in nearby Sand's Quarry, where they often met up with island teens. A sign of increasing camaraderie was when, after a dip in the East Boston Quarry, the camp boys discovered a prankster had hidden their clothes. Quite a few were late for supper that night.

Recreational activities included baseball games umpired by the local minister, Mr. Mitchell, as well as dances. According to one of the counselors, the local teens were initially afraid that the visiting Quakers "might be too religiously minded to indulge in such irrelevant activities as dancing."

However, as Bill Carey reported, the Saturday-night dances in the town hall became "a meaningful weekly point of contact with the citizenry." He remembers that a local dance favorite was the Lady of the Lake, "a distant relative of the Virginia Reel."

One night, a dispute arose among the campers when the boys alleged that some girls were "egging on" the town boys, only to give them the "stop sign" later in the evening. During the ensuing discussion, the son of a prominent Quaker was quoted as saying, "You make me so angry that I would punch you on the nose if I were not a Quaker." The campers "thrashed things out," and it was agreed that limits would be set on "local swains."

As the summer progressed, the staff found it a challenge to keep the campers busy. A staff member wrote, "Our camp tends all too easily to develop into a compromise between a work camp and a summer resort."

When some of the boys began to take on odd jobs after hours, a potentially awkward situation was created, since in doing so they were taking income away from islanders. After some discussion, it was decided to create a pool of the wages, which would be "devoted to some useful end," presumably to help out island families.

Although German submarines prowled the Maine coast, Carey said the prevailing attitude was not fear. "Submarines weren't likely to waste torpedoes or ammunition on lobster boats," he said.

Nevertheless, for teenagers on a Maine island in the summer of 1943, the war was never far from their thoughts. The Vinalhaven doctor was an Englishwoman on crutches whose legs had been crushed in the London Blitz. And 16 months after that island summer, Carey would be serving on a tanker in the Pacific.

At one point, there was a discussion among the campers about pacifism, and it became quite heated. In the end, it was agreed that those who were not pacifists learned much from those who were.

As the summer drew to a close one camper wrote, "In a world in which such horrible activities as war and race massacres are going on, we are fortunate in being able to serve by loving and helping our neighbors on this beautiful, invigorating island." ♦

Harry Gratwick is a lifelong summer resident of Vinalhaven and the author of seven books, the most recent of which is The Maritime Marauder of Revolutionary Maine, Captain Henry Mowat, *published in March.*

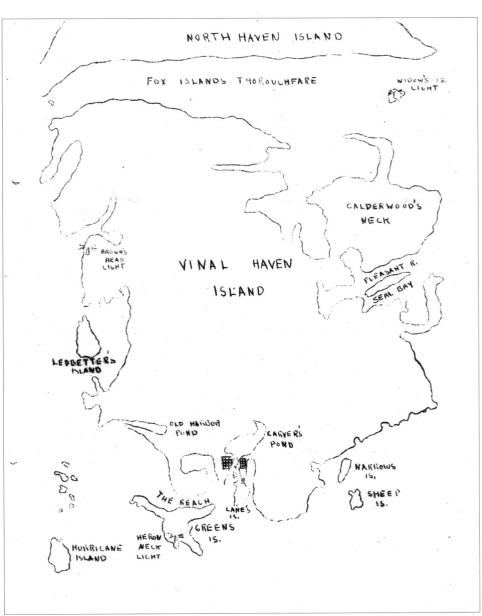

A map of Vinalhaven illustrated for the camp log

Counting Empty Houses Come Winter

Affordable housing finds a foothold on Maine's islands

BY ANNIE MURPHY

Tiffany Tate knows the frustration of looking for affordable housing on an island where all real estate is expensive and rentals are hard to come by. She was raised in Washington County, but Tate's family originally hails from Great Cranberry Isle; her grandfather built boats and was the Beal part of Beal and Bunker, which still runs the mailboat and ferry service.

After a complicated time living Downeast, including dozens of moves, Tate came to Great Cranberry in mid-2014 as a single mother, along with her five-year-old son, John. She was looking for more stability and a sense of community. And she was happy to find an islander willing to rent a summer cottage to her at far below the market rate. But when the cold weather arrived in the fall, Tate realized she had no options for winter housing.

"I was calling people, literally knocking on doors, asking, 'Would it be possible to rent this house for the winter?' It was a straight 'Nope,' or 'Yep, it's winterized, but we're not renting it,' or, 'Nope, not renting it,'" she said.

"It's their house, and of course that's their right. But if you walk up the road in the wintertime, you'll just see empty house, empty house. Someone home. Then empty house, empty house, empty house."

Tiffany Tate in front of her rent-controlled house on Great Cranberry Island SCOTT SELL

If you walk up the road in the wintertime, you'll just see empty house, empty house. Someone home. Then empty house, empty house, empty house . . .

This is the paradox of living year-round on an island in Maine: Housing is everywhere, but very few homes are affordable, or available to year-round residents.

Summer residents own much of island property; they pay taxes, put money into the local economy, and contribute in many more intangible ways. But the popularity of islands as sites for second homes has also translated into property values out of step with Maine's economy. Combine that with geographic isolation and the high cost of living, and it's increasingly hard for locals and young families to be part of island communities. Watching year-round populations fall, yet eager to remain viable communities, places like Great Cranberry are searching for ways to attract permanent residents, and affordable housing is always at the top of the list.

It was this context that gave shape to the Cranberry Isles Realty Trust, or CIRT. Founded in the late 1990s, the organization has grown from a few acres of donated land to five houses—four on Great Cranberry, and one on Islesford (Little Cranberry)—with a board, a general manager, a caretaker, and a bookkeeper. It was CIRT that eventually rented a winterized place to Tiffany Tate. For year-round residents on many of Maine's islands, similar organizations may be their best shot at preserving a way of life.

~

The night before I visited Great Cranberry, coastal Maine got its first true snowstorm of the season, knocking out power all along the coast, including on Great Cranberry. In the morning the ground was covered in a slick of ice, and the air had turned both damp and biting; with the exception of a woman in pink ballet flats and a thin blazer, everyone on the mailboat wore hooded sweatshirts, insulated canvas jackets, and winter boots. A baker from Bar Harbor sat across from me, bundled up to visit her sister and brother-in-law, who is a builder and caretaker.

She estimated that he looked after a total of 30 houses, and as we approached the dock, she began to point them out: neat, traditional places with steep roofs, their sides mostly finished in gray shingles or white clapboard.

"That one, that one. That one, too. Pretty much all of those." Her arm made a broad arc to indicate a whole line of homes along the shore.

I waited at the dock for a few minutes, and soon 32-year-old Tiffany Tate pulled up in a creaking Trans Am. The car was a shimmery robin's egg blue, and it was a few years older than she. Its passenger door was jammed shut. Tate jumped out. She seemed sturdy and somewhat delicate, too, with cropped brown hair and a careful smile.

Gesturing to me to climb across the driver's seat, she swept away clothes, shards of tree bark, and a red backpack. Three days earlier, Tate had moved into one of the rent-controlled houses that CIRT had agreed to rent to her, and was still using the car to haul her belongings there, including multiple loads of firewood, which she'd been piling into the passenger seat and balancing on the hood of the car.

In her living room, we sat in front of a woodstove on stools and drank coffee with hazelnut creamer. Along with other staples like toilet paper, pasta, and rice, she orders the coffee and creamers from Walmart or Amazon and has them shipped to the town dock. Any perishables require a trip to Southwest Harbor, or higher prices at the island store.

The room was full of the thin, silvery light of early winter. Other than us, the stove, the stools, her clothes, and a few groceries scattered in the kitchen, the place was largely empty; her son was with his dad on Islesford—he and Tate have a friendly relationship, and share custody—and all the furniture for this house was still stored in its basement. Tate said she'd planned to move the pieces upstairs bit by bit. She'd been doing a lot of sitting, just trying to get used to being on her own in the empty space.

"I'm not used to being alone, or houses that are quiet," she said. "CIRT is really a godsend. It's making it possible for my child to have a normal life."

When we spoke about where she's from, she described an absent father, her mother's problems with addiction, and a tangled list of hard living situations. She also talked about how important her son is to her, the raw beauty of the Maine coast, a sense of gratitude for having learned the skills she's built a life out of, like blueberry raking, wreath

Tiffany and Tabasco, one of her chickens SCOTT SELL

making, periwinkle collecting, clamming, scalloping, hunting, music, art, and writing—and the feeling that she's finally found a home.

"I wasn't raised here, but it's where my heart is; I guess that's the best way to put it. Here I'm close to my son, and I'm close to my family's roots. My mother's buried in the cemetery up the street. My grandfather's buried on the island. That's what it's about for me."

Tate stood, turned her back to me, and lifted her shirt to show a giant phoenix tattooed across her shoulders.

"I got this when I moved away from Washington County," she said, pulling down her shirt and returning to her stool. "It's about rebirth. Growing stronger, and all of that."

She grinned.

"Of course, it's also the Trans Am symbol. I mean, come on."

We finished our coffee and bundled up for the snow. When I asked Tate for directions to the next interview, she

I wasn't raised here, but it's where my heart is; I guess that's the best way to put it.

pointed at the house next door, then drove off for another load of belongings, the back end of the Trans Am fishtailing gracefully across the ice.

∼

Phil Whitney lives in his grandparents' old house, which he inherited and moved into with his wife, Karin, after decades of working overseas for the state department.

The Walls Family SARAH McCRACKEN

It was clear he'd been eager to return, and that he's stayed busy ever since. Sitting in his cozy living room, surrounded by blankets and family photos, Whitney talked about being part of many of the island's organizations, including CIRT, the logic behind making affordable housing available—and why islands like Great Cranberry truly need the young families living in the CIRT houses.

"In the 1980s, prices along the coast of Maine skyrocketed, and never really looked back," he said. "So if islands were going to avoid becoming entirely summer residences, something had to be done to provide year-round housing for average people. Now it's grown into the idea that we should be looking for people who not only need affordable housing, but can also bring useful skills to the island. Especially families with school-aged kids."

According to Whitney, any islander knows that a thriving school is key to attracting and keeping families as year-round residents. Although the school on Great Cranberry "ran out" of kids in 2000, when I visited, eight school-aged children were living on-island—and five of them were in CIRT houses. There are plans to reopen the school, and residents approved a $450,000 budget for repairs and remodeling.

Around noon, Karin Whitney emerged from the kitchen with fried-egg sandwiches cooked atop a woodstove, then disappeared to deal with a water issue caused by the power outage.

Phil Whitney wants to see Great Cranberry grow, but says island life isn't for everyone.

"Some people just aren't cut out to be surrounded by water and to live with just fifty or sixty other people all winter. Let's put it that way."

During the summer, Whitney helps run a shuttle that brings people from one end of the island to the other. He speaks to hundreds of day-trippers, and says that when they come in July and August, many of them claim that it's a paradise, and that they'd love to live on-island all year. So he sits and talks with them some more.

"I say, 'Do you realize what it's like in January? When you have no generator and the power goes out? Have you thought of what you'll do for work here?'" He smiles. "When I get through, the percentage of people who want to live out here has narrowed considerably."

Even those who end up happy on the island waver.

When Jen Walls and her husband, Ben, decided to move into another one of the CIRT houses, Jen felt like backing out at the last minute.

"I went over to my girlfriend's house the day before; I said 'Call Craigslist, call my family, call my friends. Find me something else. Anything!'" she told me. "We didn't have any money saved. We just had no idea what we were heading into."

Walls has curly dark hair and wears glasses, and the day we met, she was bundled up in a peacoat, since the power was out. Though Ben has family in Otter Creek, near Bar Harbor, they'd been raising their three daughters in Southern Maine, and were eager for a change. Rent was too high, and their neighborhood in Biddeford felt so unsafe that their oldest daughter, Marla, didn't like to leave the house.

"There was a lot of drug use and crime. Just in our building there was a rape, a burglary, and two meth labs. Every morning we'd wake up and just smell pot and cigarettes," said Walls.

"On the way to visit the island, she said she wasn't coming if we moved out. But on the way back, she was like, 'We are definitely moving there!,'" said her mother.

Everyone I spoke with told me it's common to have a strong reaction to the island. Ingrid Gaither works at the local store, and first came out after seeing an ad in *The Working Waterfront* while she and her husband Ric were exploring Maine. They immediately fell in love with the island, yet they moved back to North Carolina after two years.

"It was what we thought it was—but not always easy," Gaither remembered. She was wearing a kerchief over her hair, and heating water in a kettle to wash dishes at the store while Ric chatted with another customer over coffee, then went to collect their son.

As far as Phil Whitney was concerned, what mattered was that the Gaithers returned.

"They called me up three or four years ago, interested in coming back," said Whitney. "The CIRT houses were occupied; a full year passed, and finally I said, 'Why don't

"I say, 'Do you realize what it's like in January? When you have no generator and the power goes out? Have you thought of what you'll do for work here?'"

So she and Ben, who'd been working as a cook, went on Craigslist, entered in their maximum rent—$800—and their minimum number of bedrooms—three—and found the CIRT listing, at $750 for a three-bedroom home.

"Everywhere else, it was so hard to find housing," she said. "I'd call, and they'd say, 'How many in your family? . . . Oh, our septic can't handle five people.' Or, 'The space isn't big enough for five people.' But when we looked at this place, [the people at CIRT] were like, 'Oh, you have *kids*.' And they were excited."

A few weeks later, the Walls family decided to move. Now that they're on-island, Ben does carpentry, and is studying to be an EMT; Jen, who's trained as a nurse, has been helping out with elderly residents and doing books for the local boatyard, while also training to be registered as an accountant, cleaning houses, and working with the historical society. And all three girls are at the school on nearby Islesford, and say they love island life—even thirteen-year-old Marla, who in spite of not liking their old neighborhood, had close friends she didn't want to leave behind.

you come up here; I'll let you stay in one of my houses on Southwest Harbor, you pay utilities. It'll give you a foothold.'"

They came up on New Year's Day, immediately got jobs on Great Cranberry, and eventually transitioned to living on the island when a CIRT house became available.

Yet finding an affordable rental is just one part of the challenge facing anyone who really wants to live on an island. What happens after working-class, year-round residents rent for a few years, and decide they want to put down roots and own a home?

"To buy property, we have to really save," says Gaither. "But we also have to coincide with someone selling their place—someone who specifically wants a year-round resident in there. We don't ask for anything free, but we just can't afford to buy in the market for summer people."

According to Whitney, CIRT also wants to offer support to year-round residents on this front, too. He says the organization has started to consider selling CIRT houses to renters, with contracts that say the new owners won't resell within a certain amount of time, and that when they do, they must keep the properties affordable, or simply sell them back to CIRT. He also mentioned that CIRT had started to try brokering sales by residents who want to see the island thrive and are willing to sell to year-round residents who don't earn a lot of money at a price they can still afford.

Ownership is a particular concern for Tiffany Tate, who, like many Mainers, makes her living by piecing together income from different jobs, and knows it will be hard to get a loan.

"Right now, the way I work, it's a blessing and a curse, because the bank looks at you and says, 'Nope, you can't show us a steady income. You keep changing jobs. Sorry.' You get laughed at. It's kind of unrealistic to imagine that I could own something out here, unless someone would directly sell me a piece of property."

Tate was planning to focus on the immediate future.

"It's just time to work, to try to save up money," she said.

"And hopefully, someday, get a place."

Phil Whitney also hopes that young islanders like Tate, and Ben and Jen Walls, and the Gaithers will eventually have an opportunity to own property, and to stay on the island.

"If we can just keep finding housing and land opportunities for younger people with the skills to be happy here, I think we can save this island."

Whitney, like Tate, has spent a lot of time walking the island, contemplating the future of Great Cranberry.

"Last winter we had forty-eight people here; this year I think we'll be up to fifty-eight," he said. "I know, because all last winter I would walk the roads at night, and count the lights on." ♦

Annie Murphy is a journalist and radio producer. Her stories are published by The Atlantic, Harper's, *National Public Radio, and others. She runs a media studio called Ruraliste.*

Islesboro 'Homecoming' Shows Range of Affordable Housing

For a divorced mother of a five-year-old, moving to the island was a kind of retreat and a kind of homecoming. Except there was no home.

Maggy Willcox, who today publishes the *Islesboro Island News*, grew up in nearby Rockport in the early 1960s, and remembers the small-town nature of the community. It was the kind of town where mothers would send their kids out the door on a summer morning and not expect to see them again until lunchtime.

So in 1990 when she found herself alone with her child, the idea of spending the summer on Islesboro was appealing.

"I just needed a change of scene," she recalled, and the island was "very much like" the small town of Rockport. "As a newly single mother, that looked very attractive. I thought, 'Okay, that's a good place to spend the summer.'"

She took a job at the food truck that operates seasonally at the ferry landing.

"It was a step back in time. It was magical," she said, and decided to stay through the winter. Her first place was "little more than a camp. It was two rooms, not really winterized, and had an outhouse, where the infamous up-island spiders would hang out. You'd bang on the door before going in."

After that, home was a summer resident's place, also not winterized. She stayed in exchange for working on the house.

"There were always these strange little deals you could work out," she recalled.

Enrolling her son in the island's highly rated school made her want to find a more permanent deal. The Islesboro Affordable Property group had formed in the early 1990s, and had completed a housing needs study and landed funding. Its first project was an eight-unit subdivision on 13 acres that had been sold at a discount by the late resident Ruthie James.

"I was one of many applicants," Willcox said, but she was chosen. The houses were designed to be owner-built, with materials precut and labeled, so "Tab A would go into Slot B." Those selected for the houses were supposed to work together to build them, and finish them in 28 weekends.

"None of that happened," she said. The blueprints were minimal, and as one family's house was finished, they concentrated on its own interior work—understandable, Willcox said—and couldn't stay with the building team. The housing group's executive director quit abruptly in the middle of the project.

By this time, Willcox was working at the post office.

A barge brings a piece of modular housing to Great Cranberry Island for installation.
COURTESY GREAT CRANBERRY ISLAND HISTORICAL SOCIETY

People would routinely offer to help work on the house on the weekend, but few turned up. Chuck Whitehouse, now deceased, offered and came through.

"He spent a year and a half with me on weekends," she said. "It was the most Christian act I have ever seen in my life."

Her ex-husband and many others took on specific projects; the island-based Central Maine Power representative "took scraps from the boards we used for walls and made me custom kitchen cabinets. I baked a lot then, and he even built a tip-out bin for my forty-pound bags of flour and sugar."

Still, there were bad moments.

"I remember sitting on my roof, nailing in boards, and sobbing," she recalled.

It's no wonder the island affordable housing group now buys modular homes.

The story has a happy ending, though. The home she now shares with her husband, Peter, a boat captain for the environmental activist group Greenpeace, is eye-pleasing with its steep pitched roof, and comfortable, with a soaring living-room ceiling balanced by an efficient galley kitchen. At 1,172 square feet, "It's what the real estate people call *cozy*," Willcox joked.

Exposed studs and sheathing planks create a warm effect, while the rigid foam insulation attached outside the sheathing means it heats easily.

Through a land-lease agreement, Willcox pays Islesboro Affordable Property just under $100 month. The nonprofit owns the land and the shared wells and septic systems. Mortgage payments are in the $500 to $700 range for most, she said. If a house is sold, the home builder gets $5,000 back for the "sweat equity," plus a percentage of the value of whatever improvements have been made (porches, decks, etc.).

Her son Sky graduated from the school—one in a class of three—so the happy ending was complete. "I'm so glad I made that commitment," Willcox said, which made his education there possible.

These days, affordable housing includes both public efforts and a more informal, island network, Willcox said. Three of the original eight remain in the subdivision; the other five have moved off-island, she said, adding, "You come here and you appear to be useful, people will go the extra mile and find you a place." ♦

—Tom Groening

The second story of the Woodland House is installed on Great Cranberry Island.
COURTESY GREAT CRANBERRY ISLAND HISTORICAL SOCIETY

Carving Out Funds for Island Affordable Housing

"AFFORDABLE" HOUSING HAS a different meaning on the islands. Thanks to their desirability for seasonal homes and the finite land available, real estate costs are significantly higher than on the mainland.

Explaining that reality to legislators who were crafting a bond aimed at helping towns build affordable houses wasn't easy, though. Genesis Community Loan Fund and the Island Institute were able to do so, and as a result, a $30 million bond package approved by Maine voters in 2010 included $2 million devoted to building affordable rental housing on year-round islands.

The rules for distributing the housing funds were crafted "for the needs of rural communities through flexible standards," remembers Greg Payne, director of the Maine Affordable Housing Coalition. Those standards were written with islands in mind, he said.

Affordable housing initiatives typically target communities with lower median incomes, Payne said. Fishermen on islands would be ineligible under those standards, however, because some of those communities have high median incomes.

The rules for grant awards took island income into consideration, as well as the smaller scale of island projects; fewer units were built, which was less efficient, but made sense in small island towns, Payne said.

Construction costs are significantly higher on islands, too, a wrinkle that normally would have had legislators leaning away from such high-cost, low-return projects. Fortunately, significant lobbying of legislators persuaded them to understand and accept the island-specific challenges.

"The Island Institute had a big role in making a great success of the subset of this bond," Payne said. He also credited Liza Fleming-Ives of Genesis.

Rental units were chosen over ownership to provide essential workforce housing, he said.

The island units built through the bond included six on Vinalhaven and two each on North Haven, Islesboro, Chebeague, Peaks, Isle au Haut, and Great Cranberry islands. ♦

—Tom Groening

THE ALLURING AND ENDURING MAINE COAST

Historic images from the Penobscot Marine Museum

SWIFT'S WINDJAMMER CRUISER, CAMDEN, MAINE
3957

THE PENOBSCOT MARINE MUSEUM'S PHOTOGRAPHIC COLLECTION IS VAST – OVERWHELMINGLY VAST . . .

. . . Lucky for me, I had the privilege of working with Kevin Johnson, the museum's photo archivist, who guided me in the right direction as we selected the group to include in this issue of *Island Journal*.

Hours and hours of looking through images in the museum's collections from the Eastern Illustrating and Publishing Co., Elmer and Ruth Montgomery, and Ed Coffin left me feeling I had seen each and every harbor of our state's coast. While they each have their unique characteristics, they all began to look the same.

I kept asking myself, what is going to engage the viewers in this folio? How am I going to tell the story of what this coast was like before my family lived here? What will give the viewer a strong sense of place? And I kept hearing one answer: People.

After pulling over 150 possible images for this folio and the exhibit that will follow at our Main Street, Rockland gallery, we narrowed it down to images that had characters with stories that transcend the barriers of time. Represented by a few key images here, the exhibit that opens June 26, "The Alluring and Enduring Maine Coast," features 30-plus photographs. Characters such as the Broiler Queen

of Belfast, a reminder of that town's chicken processing past, craftsmen working granite architectural elements on Vinalhaven, and the barber on a boat out of Thomaston, each call to the viewer from the two dimensional space and ask us to imagine their lives and listen to their stories. I particularly like the women in all their finery and a girl with her doll, putting out a spread on Matinicus. I can only imagine what it felt like in all those clothes and hats, offering a picnic for the fisherman on the rocky beach.

This is the first time we have hosted an exhibition of historic images from such a broad geographic range, from down the coast to Eastport and out to Matinicus.

We invite you to see the exhibit to learn more about that broiler queen and the others, as each image will have an informative caption researched by museum volunteers. And yes, each has a story to tell.

For more information about the Archipelago Fine Arts Gallery exhibit in Rockland, please visit www.thearchipelago.net.

— *Lisa Mossel Vietze, Archipelago director*

North Haven and Vinalhaven ferry, 1956

Vinalhaven, 1900

Aboard a vessel out of Thomaston, 1895

Rockland, 1951

Aboard a vessel out of Boothbay, 1895

A shore-side picnic on Matinicus Island, 1898

Belfast's Broiler Queen of 1949, an honor bestowed at the annual Broiler Festival

Criehaven, 1900

Aboard a vessel out of Boothbay, 1895

Eastport, 1924

EASTPORT

73

AN OYSTER STORY

The source of that slurpy, salty goodness is the 'taste of place'

BY CATHERINE SCHMITT

At three in the afternoon on a Friday in January, all the seats are full at Eventide Oyster Company in Portland. Outside, the temperatures are plummeting, but inside the sun shines through the wall of windows, illuminating the small space.

Oysters, ten varieties from Maine and another seven "from away," all grown in carefully chosen environments, are on display in an ice-filled granite basin. The bearded guy with a pom-pommed ski hat shucking oysters, the capable bartender, the nimble servers—all stay in the background. Here, oysters are front and center.

Each variety of oyster—that craggy and somewhat mysterious shellfish—has a story to tell. But every oyster story must first include a bit of background. What are oysters? Where did they come from? Why are they here, now?

The Eastern oyster, *Crassostrea virginica*, is native to coastal waters from the Gulf of St. Lawrence to the Gulf of Mexico. Oyster populations in Maine have fluctuated with climate shifts and rising sea levels (evidence: giant fossil oyster shells dredged up from around the Gulf of Maine). The native Wabanaki people ate tons of oysters (evidence: huge piles of discarded shells or "middens" along the coast, especially in the Damariscotta River area).

This evidence, combined with the fact that the Ira C. Darling marine laboratory facility was located on the banks of the Damariscotta, that ancient oyster river, led

*Why then the world's mine Oyster,
which I, with sword will open.*

—*Shakespeare,* The Merry Wives of Windsor

*Abel LaBelle bags oysters in
Salt Pond on North Haven.*
SETH MACY

Herb Hidu and other University of Maine scientists to experiment with culturing oysters in the 1970s. Their legacy can be seen today in the 50 or so oyster farms in Maine producing millions of oysters a year.

> *An oyster is an island unto itself*
> *full of rocks and earth,*
> *tide-swept marsh and rain-washed forest,*
> *salt and sun:*
> *the taste of a place*
> *in*
> *one*
> *bite.*

From Taunton Bay near Sullivan in Hancock County to the Piscataqua River at the New Hampshire line, Maine's oyster growers ply their trade with a commitment that borders on the obsessive. By nature, oyster farmers are curious, adventurous. They are tinkerers and experimenters. They are always busy: trying out new gear, moving oysters around, evaluating shell shape and meat quality, packing, delivering, selling, talking oysters. They don't like to be bored.

Fortunately for all of us—growers, sellers, consumers, writers—oysters are never boring. I have had the privilege of visiting a number of oyster farms during the years I've been writing about Maine and our seafood. Most recently, I went out to North Haven to see Adam Campbell, who grows oysters in Salt Pond.

Like some other people who get into oyster farming, Campbell was a commercial fisherman in search of another way to make a living on the water. He is part of the "second wave" of oyster farmers in Maine, who are learning from the first wave, the graduate students of Herb Hidu, who

Ready for shucking at Eventide Oyster Company in Portland
HEETH GRANTHAM

went on to start the first commercial oyster farms in the state.

After 15 years as a shellfish farmer, oysters have turned into "a nice little gig" for Campbell, he says, as he continues to work as a lobsterman. Lobstering is more lucrative, but oysters provide "a great way for me to make part of my living," said Campbell. "I wouldn't give it up."

We ate oysters because they were there.
We ate them until they were gone.
Then we found a way to grow them, and put them back
so we could eat them again.

Part of the science of oyster farming is finding a place where oysters will grow, where the water-flow and salinity and temperature are just right, with enough algae for the oysters to eat. The bottom should be somewhere between muddy and rocky. The oyster is a creature of the estuary, the waters in between fresh and salt, the part of the ocean that most of us know, the familiar sea we can see from land, the coastal zone.

Taunton Bay
Frenchman Bay
Blue Hill
Bagaduce River
North Haven
Weskeag
Meduncook
Medomak
John's River
Damariscotta (Pemaquid, Glidden Point)
Sheepscot
New Meadows River (Winter Point)
Maquoit Bay (Flying Point)
Harraseeket
Casco Bay (Basket Island, Pine Point)
Scarborough (Pine Point, Nonesuch)
Webhannet
Piscataqua

Feeding and growth are both tied to temperature. Oysters enter a dormant state below 40 degrees; they can even withstand freezing for short periods of time. In the 20th century, when state and university scientists were trying to start a new industry, Maine waters were too cold for oysters to spawn on their own or grow very fast.

Not anymore.

In some places, oysters now take only two years instead of four to grow to market size (two to three inches).

Warmer waters are expanding areas where oyster culture is feasible.

A few years ago, it got so warm that Adam Campbell's oysters spawned on their own. Some of the juvenile oysters settled on rocks and ledges in the tidal flats below the pond. Seeing how well they grew, Campbell used the new site for some of his cultured "seed" (oyster farmers buy their oysters from a handful of hatcheries around the state). The first year he and his crew estimated 25,000 oysters would

Eating oysters is a synesthetic experience, the sense of taste concomitant with place.

grow there, but the harvest turned up more than 85,000.

Now Campbell uses the pond as a nursery, and the tidal inlet (he calls it "Oyster Nirvana") as a grow-out site. He mostly harvests in the winter, hiring a crew to push shelves of ice out of the way to reach the oysters, which sit on the bottom. Campbell rides the ferry to the mainland with his oysters, delivering them to Jess's Market in Rockland and J.P.'s Shellfish in Portland.

He has learned to stick to his schedule. "When you say you're going to show up with oysters, you better show up with oysters."

Eating oysters is a synesthetic experience, the sense of taste concomitant with place. Oysters eat by filtering seawater. As water and particles (algae, mostly, but also other bits of detritus) move along the gill surface, the oyster selects some particles to ingest, and ejects the rest. How an oyster does this isn't totally clear, but likely has something to do with the chemistry between the particle surface and proteins in the mucus covering the feeding organ. Digested, the food deconstructs into protein, iron, selenium, zinc, and other trace elements combined in proportions unique to the oyster's home.

And so oysters soak up their surroundings, synthesizing land and sea; the red clay of the upper Damariscotta, eelgrass in Taunton Bay, reversing falls of the Bagaduce, shallow sunlit waters of North Haven's Salt Pond, and the circulation of Casco Bay are captured in their respective oysters.

An island in its own ocean surrounded by shell, every

*Adam Campbell of
North Haven Oyster Company*
SETH MACY

oyster tastes different. Describing the taste, however, is harder than describing wine, or art. Even the best ekphrasis fails to convey the experience.

> *muddy*
> *earthy*
> *mineral*
> *grassy*
> *briny*
> *salty*
> *cold*
> *clean*
> *bright*

Maybe words for the flavor are so elusive because eating oysters is about more than tasting oysters.

In her classic *Consider the Oyster*, M. F. K. Fisher wrote, "[O]ften the place and time help make certain food what it becomes."

Place matters, obviously. Timing matters, too, and yet timing doesn't matter. Whatever the season or time of day, oysters transform the routine into celebration, the mundane into ceremony. Perhaps it's the element of danger—eating raw oysters always carries some risk, although Maine has strict standards for harvesting and selling shellfish. Still, it's best to eat raw oysters at a place that specializes in the ritual, or has an association with an oyster farm.

As successful as Eventide has been since it opened in 2012—in fact, it's being expanded, as chefs Andrew Taylor and Mike Wiley add to their block of award-winning restaurants— not everyone is familiar with Maine oysters, or how to eat them.

"A lot of people let us choose for them, and that's fun," said server Janet Webber, who grew up in Boothbay on the Damariscotta River, and so is familiar with the industry that more and more people are getting to know.

Another dozen down, and I'm getting to know something, too: with oysters, the story writes itself. ♦

Catherine Schmitt is the communications director for the Maine Sea Grant program at the University of Maine, and the author of A Coastal Companion: A Year in the Gulf of Maine from Cape Cod to Canada.

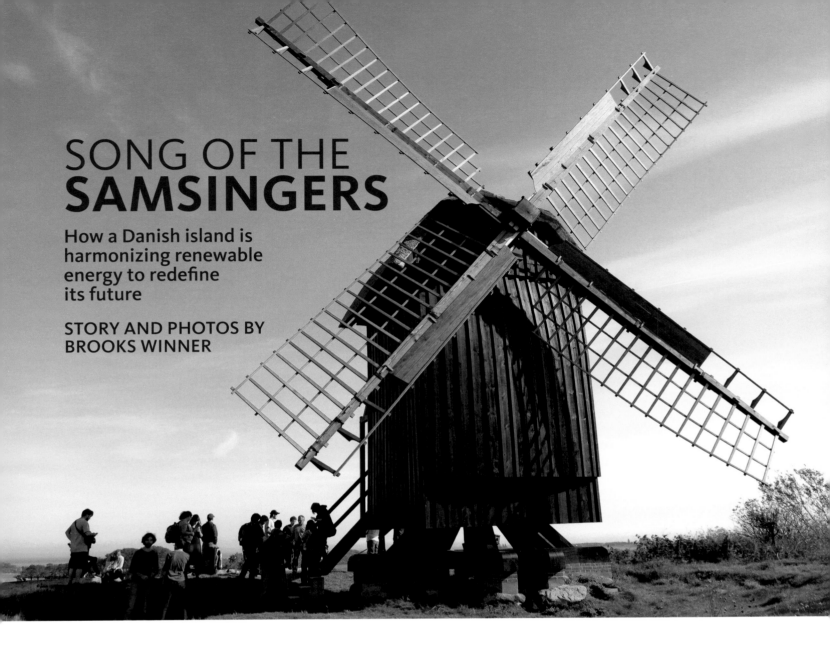

SONG OF THE SAMSINGERS

How a Danish island is harmonizing renewable energy to redefine its future

STORY AND PHOTOS BY BROOKS WINNER

Landing on Samsø Island, part of Denmark, we were greeted by a kind of rock star.

"Hello! My name is Søren," exclaimed the man. "I am the lead singer of the Samsingers," he smiled, echoing a local pun (the residents of the island are known as "Samsingers"). Søren Hermansen was our host and tour guide, and though he doesn't play or sing in a band, he is indeed a rock star, traveling the world as a spokesman for community energy projects, telling the story of how Samsø, his hometown, is building its own sustainable energy future.

Over the last decade, the Danish island of Samsø has become a beacon of sustainability throughout Europe and beyond. Remarkably, with a mix of community and privately owned wind farms (on land and offshore), straw-fired heating plants, electric vehicles, and solar panels, Samsø now produces more energy from renewables than it consumes, making it one of the first carbon-negative communities in the world.

In September 2014, five Maine islanders traveled to Samsø to learn how the community became world-renowned as an example of such smart energy development. The islanders were Marian Chioffi of Monhegan, Nate Johnson of Long Island in Casco Bay, Tom McAloon of Swan's Island, Sam Saltonstall of Peaks Island, and Patrick Trainor of Vinalhaven. They were joined by 18 students and faculty from Bar Harbor's College of the Atlantic and two representatives from the Island Institute's Community Energy Program (myself included).

All are participants in the Collaborative for Island

BECAUSE THE STAKES WERE HIGH BACK HOME, THEY NEEDED MORE THAN WORDS OF INSPIRATION. THEY WERE LOOKING FOR SOLID, PRACTICAL INSIGHTS.

Energy Research and Action, or CIERA, a new partnership between the college and the Island Institute, supported by the Fund for Maine Islands. Over the course of our two-week visit, we explored the island, meeting the people who are leading this energy revolution and making it Denmark's "renewable energy island."

≈

The Maine delegation was there to listen and learn from Hermansen and his colleagues. Our group was different from many that visit because we had two weeks on the island, much more time to explore than most who come for a day or two, and because we planned to use the knowledge we'd gain to help shape energy initiatives when we returned home.

While Samsingers are not especially well known for their musical skills, after a few days at the Energy Academy, we began to feel as if we were watching a well-choreographed song-and-dance routine. Søren's stories about the process by which Samsø became Denmark's model of sustainable energy were fine-tuned, funny, and engaging. The narrative that he and his colleagues had crafted was one of unity, optimism, and change.

But the Maine islanders were looking for more than that. They wanted to know how it had been done, and what they could bring home to apply on their own islands. They were looking for some best practices, new approaches, and fresh ideas. Instead, what they were hearing seemed to be a well-rehearsed story. Because the stakes were high back home, they needed more than words of inspiration. They were looking for solid, practical insights.

Maine's island communities face significant challenges related to energy and climate change. For example, Monhegan residents pay upwards of $0.70 per kilowatt-hour, one of the highest electric rates in the country, a challenge that contributes to the high cost of living on the island. This has become one of the biggest threats to the island remaining a year-round community.

Swan's Island Electric Cooperative has operated for more than a year with a volunteer general manager and no full-time line worker, struggling to maintain its aging infrastructure with declining revenues and one of the smallest memberships of any independent electric cooperative in the United States.

Adding to the challenges are disturbing signs of climate change—sea-level rise, increasingly powerful storms, acidifying oceans—all pressing issues for islanders who are, by nature and necessity, acutely aware of changes in their environment. Far more than a mere academic exercise, the trip to Denmark was an opportunity for the CIERA participants to soak up as much as they could, and to envision fruitful solutions for problems widely recognized in their communities.

After the first week of tours and introductory presentations, the islanders were champing at the bit, ready to find the good stuff. Here was a unique opportunity to take a multi-week master class with the sultan of sustainability. They were not about to waste it.

≈

"Let me stop you there," one of the Mainers interjected during a presentation about how businesses on Samsø had embraced the community's energy-efficiency efforts. "This is a great story, but we want to know how this all happened. What were the incentives? What were the policies that made this possible? How did you sell this to the community?"

The presenter, one of Søren's colleagues, looked a bit puzzled at the question. We were asking him to go deeper, to give us more than the quick show-and-tell that many who attend the Energy Academy get. We had time to investigate further and dissect the actual strategies and policies that Samsø has used to achieve such impressive results.

From there, the real exploration began. The Mainers asked tough questions. The Samsingers responded with direct, honest answers. As the CIERA participants traveled around the island, talking to as many people as they could

CIERA participants in an Energy Academy brainstorming session

in the remaining week, the gracious Danes welcomed them warmly into their homes and businesses.

Farmers who had invested in the wind project offered contrasting views. Some loved "their" turbines, while others expressed disappointment in the financial returns. Homeowners who had retrofitted their old island homes with thick insulation and energy-efficient electric heat pumps explained that the Danish government offered a special electric rate that made heat pumps a worthy successor to fossil-fuel systems.

The Mainers also met with a leader of the municipal government to hear about the island's ambitious plans for rolling out electric vehicles across the island and replacing its diesel ferryboat with one powered by locally produced biogas.

When they quizzed Søren about specific incentives offered by the Danish government to promote renewable energy development, he explained that much of the $80 million spent to build the energy projects on Samsø came from subsidies or large corporate investments. Multinational oil and gas giant Royal Dutch Shell even chipped in for the offshore wind project.

By taking the time to dig into these crucial details, we got a better sense of what had worked, what hadn't, and what was worth bringing back home. We had interrupted the song of the Samsingers, but in doing so we were able to more closely examine the instruments and the composition of the piece, allowing us to learn the best of what our maestros had to offer.

Since returning to their own islands, CIERA participants have started to digest the lessons learned from the trip and to integrate them into their own island energy projects. While each came away with something slightly different, there were important common themes that emerged.

Tom McAloon, the semiretired utility engineer from

Søren Hermansen, left, with the author atop one of Samsø's wind turbines

Swan's Island, observes that despite the narrative about local engagement and investment, national incentives actually played a major part in setting the Samsingers up for success—even though those national incentives didn't always work as intended.

"There may be clever ways to take the Danish example and leapfrog it," he said, suggesting that Maine islands could learn from the challenges the Danes have faced as renewable energy pioneers.

McAloon has examined a menu of options for the Swan's Island Electric Cooperative to consider as it looks for ways to continue to provide safe, reliable, and affordable electricity to its members. These options could include new technologies like electric vehicles or air-source heat pumps, but they could also include rethinking the way the cooperative operates. This "menu" is helping to inform discussions about the community's energy future and how to address high energy costs on the island.

"I was most impressed by the community investment process and the model used by Samsingers to implement renewable energy projects," said Nate Johnson, the Long Island native who works as an environmental engineer for one of the world's leading tidal energy companies. Samsingers were allowed to buy shares of the wind turbines built on the island, a strategy that helped to build support for the project throughout the community.

As he investigates options for building a renewable energy demonstration project, Johnson plans to look for ways to engage his community through similar approaches. "There may not be a track record of energy projects on Long Island, but there is a basis for other community-led initiatives, like the effort to secede from Portland, which could provide a foundation for future projects," he said.

Perhaps the most valuable part of the trip for the Mainers, however, was the opportunity to connect with other islanders in a new and inspirational setting. When the CIERA participants get together, they share notes on everything from energy costs to entertainment.

"It was a wonderful experience to meet islanders from other Maine islands and Samsø," said Patrick Trainor of Vinalhaven. "We shared stories of the higher cost of living on islands. We shared our love of island communities, the depth of our islands' histories, and their stunning natural beauty."

Given the space and time to explore shared energy challenges with their peers, the islanders could embrace new roles in shaping their islands' energy futures and dare to dream big.

~

On our last day on the Danish island, after we had said most of our good-byes, we had one last meeting at the Energy Academy. A group of islanders from around Europe—members of the European Union's "Smilegov" (smart multilevel governance) initiative—had converged on the island to discuss their plans to meet the EU's ambitious goals for greenhouse gas reduction, renewable energy production, and energy efficiency. Søren invited us to join them.

While the Mainers could easily have felt overwhelmed by the group that included representatives from islands of over a million people and communities already implementing ambitious and innovative energy projects, instead, they felt right at home. All of them jumped right into the discussion, talking with government leaders from Malta, Cyprus, and the Orkney Islands of Scotland, sharing their experience and soaking up the insights from their European counterparts.

Later that afternoon, we said *farvel* (good-bye) to our hosts and hopped aboard the ferry to begin the journey back to Maine. Our two-week jam session with the leader of the Samsingers had ended, but the CIERA participants left with new ideas and new material, energized and ready to get to work creating their own energy masterpieces. ♦

You can follow the progress of the CIERA project on the blog at http://fundformaineislands.org/category/ciera/.

Brooks Winner is a community energy associate at the Island Institute, publisher of Island Journal.

The Ballad of the Three Green Waves

BY RUTH MOORE

No, I ain't got no dorymate.
I goes by myself, alone.
I can't have nobody gorming round
Anything that's my own.

I ain't married and never will.
I come when I likes, and go.
Folks and fussing's all very well
For them as likes um so.

When I puts out to haul my traps
In a good rip-staving sea,
There ain't a soul on the face of the earth
Worrying after me.

Now, there was my brother, years ago,
Got him a wife and kid,
Worried and wore himself plumb out
Being easy in what he did.

We was hauling traps outside one time,
When it come on a howling blow
Cold as a dog and the wind northeast,
Thicker un tar with snow.

Them was the days when we worked with sails,
They warn't no engines then.
I had a peapod and steered with an oar,
But that warn't enough for Hen.

He had a dory rigged up with a mast,
And a mainsail without no jib,
So's he could set in the stern and steer
With a tiller hugged in his rib.

Well, the wind was coming, and Hen shoots up—
One eye on the line of foam—
"Jarp!" he yells, "What in hell'll I do?
I've left my compass home!"

Thinks I to myself, "You goddam fool,
Fixed up like a blooming yacht!
So blasted careful—" I hove him mine.
"Ketch!" says I, and he caught.

Hen warn't no good when it come to fog.
Or snow-squalls thicker 'n sin;
But I never see the rampagen yit
I could lose my bearings in.

Down she come and she was a bitch.
I squat on the end of my oar
And headed into her hard's I could
And let her roar.

I warn't troubled. What'd I care?
I never had no wife.
And as for dying, well, they's them
That's troubled all their life.

"Holler, you damned old slut," says I.
"Holler, and bust your lung.
If I get scared of your going's-on,"
Says I, "May I be hung!"

And I sung all the hymn tunes I ever knowed,
Cause them's the kind you can roar.
I never heard a word I sung,
But my throat got kind of sore.

Then I looks behind and I see three waves,
Following fast as sin,
Each of um reaching his whiskers out
To grab and wrostle me in.

Thinks I to myself, If them ketch me,
(Glory, amen, amen)
They's fish that'll have good feed tonight,
(Revive us again, again).

— POEM —

From Cold as a Dog and the Wind Northeast, Ballads by Ruth Moore, *reprinted by permission of Blackberry Books, Nobleboro, Maine. Special thanks to Gary Lawless.*

The first one, he was dark and deep,
And smooth as a coffee cup;
And the next one, he was a slash of foam
Like a kettle boiling up.

But the last one, he was the whole green sea,
And he had a wicked eye,
And slobbering jaws; and "He's the one
As is longing for me," thinks I.

So I spits out over the peapod's stern,
And I turns my back on the sea,
And in a minute, I feels the rise
Of the first one under me.

The first one lifted us up and up,
Soft as a sea of oil,
The next one bit at me going by,
I could see his innards boil.

Six fathom deep in the trough he made,
I looks through the glass-green sea,
Clear as a bell through that last wave,
As was towering over me.

The bare black bottom spread beneath,
For miles and miles around,
And school on school of big sea fish
Looked up without a sound.
Their eyes were buttons off dead men's coats,
Shiny and cold and still;
And the first time ever in all my life
I felt my innards chill.

For whiles I was looking, down come Hen,
Sunk like a chunk of lead
Large as life and as natural,
Only I seen he was dead.

Them big sea fish, they swayed aside,
With a little swirl and a swish,
And then I never see Hen no more
Only the backs of fish;

And the snake-weeds waving up and down,
Their ends all crimped and curled—
The trough between two big he-waves
Is the stillest place in the world.

Then foam was in my mouth like hair,
And a howling in my ears,
And I swum in the middle of that there wave
For a hundred thousand years;

Till I bumped my head on the back-shore beach,
Spewed up like a goddam pill,
And that old wave went reeling back,
Laughing fit to kill.

Now, a dory's made to stand the seas
Of any kind of a gale,
But all that we ever found of Hen
Was the top of his dinner-pail.

I maintained then and I maintains now
That Hen would of saved his life,
If his mind had been on steering his boat
Instead of on his wife.

"Oh, if anything come to me," says Hen,
What would my poor wife *do?*"
And I never cared a hoot in hell,
By gorry, and I come through.

No, when I goes, I goes alone,
Through fire, water and paint,
I ain't got a soul to worry 'bout me,
And I don't care if I ain't.

A TIDAL JOY RIDE

Boys find a surprising third for their Vinalhaven outing

BY PHIL CROSSMAN

ILLUSTRATIONS BY SCOTT NASH

GLANCING DOWN HE COULD EASILY MAKE OUT A LARGE SHADOW, MUCH LARGER THAN HIMSELF, NEARLY TOUCHING—**AND THEN TOUCHING**—HIS LEG.

Elias and Drew donned the life jackets they'd selected from the wide assortment found in the barn and scurried out onto the line of rocks and ledges that constituted a little jetty at the head of the rapids. Twelve-year-old Elias had been coming to Vinalhaven from Illinois with his folks for a dozen summers, but his friend Drew, also twelve, was enjoying his first trip. For that matter, it was Drew's first solo trip of any consequence outside Chicago, where he lived with his folks and went to school.

Elias's family rented a saltwater farm on seven gently rolling and magnificent acres that fronted on the southeast shore of Vinal Cove. The big, comfortable farmhouse and nearby barn sat naturally on a modest rise overlooking the cove. Once an active saltwater farm, it's now a pastoral retreat enjoyed not only by the appreciative seasonal owners and their guests, but also by the islanders, to whom those owners have graciously extended permission for such things as a fall carnival, musical events, auctions, fund-raisers, and so forth.

For years, too, the picturesque farm has been the first choice of many a celebrant, newlyweds in particular. Photos of brides and grooms gazing adoringly at one another under an arbor facing west toward the cove, or north over the rolling little meadows, or in the big timber-frame barn after an indoor ceremony are scattered far and wide around the country.

The boys shared a bedroom on the second floor of the big rambling farmhouse, and the enchanting scent that saltwater ways dispense now and then breathed wakefulness into them each early morning, fueling their enthusiasm for what each new day might offer. Sounds of competing gulls amplified the anticipation, particularly if the tide was out and the flats exposed.

If the tide was not fully out, but on its way, the gulls and terns would be diving in and out up at the rapids, at the north end of the property where Vinal Cove quenches its thirst twice a day with each incoming tide, having expelled an identical quantity just a few hours earlier. At this restricted waterway between the cove and Winter Harbor, its patron estuary, the outgoing tide creates substantial rapids—fairly clear of rocks and obstacles—extending downstream for a hundred yards or so.

During this vacation the boys had been converging at this juncture to ride the rapids nearly every day, about two hours after high tide had turned. Then, for several exciting hours, the water was moving at full force but afforded enough depth to allow them to avoid the rocks beneath.

Of course, the outgoing tide was simultaneously rolling seaward in Winter Harbor, and its water level was dropping, too, so riding the rapids too long after the tide had turned would not have provided enough depth for the safe passage of two boys hurtling gleefully downstream.

On one of those days the boys headed for the rapids at about noon, with Elias's watchful mom, as always, observing from shore. Their arrival coincided with a carnal frenzy of some tiny critters, maybe herring, out in the harbor just beyond the rapids. Whatever that critter was, its activity attracted a handful of predators not far from the rapids, but far from the trio's attention.

While Elias's mom urged caution from the sidelines—though less urgently with each passing day, since there'd been no mishaps or injuries—the boys scrambled toward their chosen launching spot. This was routine now—no lingering apprehension—and Elias flung himself confidently into the rushing water.

As soon as the current jerked him around so he faced downstream, he sensed an extraordinary, startling, and unexpected warmth underwater next to his right side. Glancing down he could easily make out a large shadow, much larger than himself, nearly touching—and then touching—his leg.

His first thought—not surprisingly for a twelve-year-old boy—was that it was a shark or some other underwater monster, but just as quickly he deduced—also remarkable for a twelve-year-old—that given the distance from deep water and the shark's customary habitat, this was unlikely.

In the next instant, a big harbor seal popped up right in front of him; its steely black head, much bigger than his own, had white stripes extending from the center of its forehead down and off to the right and left, on either side of its V-shaped nostrils. These were contracting and expanding, the latter effort enveloping Elias's face with a pungent odor, not altogether unpleasant but unmistakably digestive.

The big creature's eyes looked inquiringly into Elias's own as the duo hurtled down the rapids—Elias facing downstream and the seal facing upstream—their heads about a foot apart, perfectly choreographed. The ride seemed to go on forever, Elias at the mercy of the current, exercising no control whatsoever, and the seal entirely otherwise, effortlessly making adjustments where necessary to keep it facing backwards.

This business of keeping its bulk a foot away from and facing the boy for the duration of the tumultuous ride presented no challenge to the playful pinniped. Watching from shore, aghast at first, Elias's mom saw the astonishment and wonder on her son's face as this miraculous adventure unfolded, and began running parallel along the shore, the better to rendezvous with him the instant the ride was over.

The thrill lasted nearly a minute, one that will certainly linger, and for the duration the seal never took his inquiring eyes off Elias's own. As the current slowed and settled into not much more than a little eddy, the boy's feet touched bottom and the seal was gone. Elias splashed toward shore, toward his mom, eager to give voice to this extraordinary experience.

Of course, she had seen it all and was no less eager herself.

Breathlessly, they blurted out the details simultaneously, and as they did, Drew, who had also seen everything, shouted out his intention to launch his own ride. Elias and his mom looked up at the head of the rapids as Drew signaled his readiness and jumped into the current.

The seal, having scurried easily back upstream during the intervening seconds for a repeat of the thrill it seemed to have enjoyed coming down with Elias, popped up as before, right in front of Drew, and gave him the same companionably breathtaking ride downstream.

This time, though, when it was over and Drew's feet touched bottom, the seal lingered. It looked at Drew and then at the others onshore. It paddled around him, at times bumping him gently until Drew tentatively reached out a hand and stroked its back as it drifted back and forth. After a few minutes it submerged and disappeared.

Drew splashed ashore to join Elias and his mom. Each blurting out his own frenzied version of events, the two boys suddenly realized that this adventure might not be over, and raced up to the top of the rapids for another dance.

Alas, the seal had apparently had enough excitement for one day, and had moved on out into Winter Harbor—presumably to find its own family and relate its own version of this fun encounter with another species. ◆

Phil Crossman lives with his wife Elaine on Vinalhaven, where he owns and operates the Tidewater Motel.

MBNA and the Midcoast Miracle

Ten years ago, the credit-card lender was bought by Bank of America, but its legacy remains

BY TOM GROENING

MBNA. Four letters that actually stood for nothing, yet oh-so-much, in the mid-1990s through 2005.

The Delaware-based credit-card lender, spun off from Maryland Bank, National Association—hence the name—dominated the Midcoast landscape for those years. From 50 jobs in Camden in 1993 to 4,500 statewide by the early 2000s, its growth here was dramatic and visible.

Some companies quietly go about their business and hope to avoid controversy and dodge media attention. They write checks to national charitable groups and stay out of local initiatives.

Not MBNA.

The company and its CEO, Charlie Cawley, were big fish in the small pond that is Maine. They introduced corporate culture to towns that had never before seen it, and sometimes, it was an uneasy marriage. In Knox and Waldo counties, MBNA's presence was at its largest and most dramatic. The phrase "800-pound gorilla" was used more than once by media pundits.

But despite what critics said—and they said a lot—as Maine staggered out of one of the worst recessions

Rockland's waterfront boardwalk, a favorite spot for locals, was built by MBNA.
ERIC WAYNE

The children's section of the Rockland Public Library was expanded with help from MBNA donations.
SCOTT SELL

in decades in the early 1990s, the jobs that MBNA offered were a shot of adrenaline to the Midcoast's anemic economy. And the corporate and personal giving—particularly on the part of Cawley—gave new meaning to the word *generosity*.

In July, ten years will have passed since Bank of America purchased MBNA and those four letters passed into history. But the company's impact remains. Many of the large office complexes built around the state, sold by Bank of America at bargain prices, are occupied by other businesses today.

Beyond the jobs and the infrastructure, MBNA may have had an even more profound hand in polishing—if not remaking—the public landscape of the Midcoast and some of Maine's islands. Education and schools, libraries, YMCAs, art museums, performance spaces, parks, and several nonprofits—including the Island Institute, publisher of *Island Journal*—were lifted up and set on new, firm foundations. It was a level of giving that recalled 19th-century donors like Carnegie and Rockefeller.

Some of what MBNA did never got reported. One small anecdote: The company paid for teachers at elementary schools to quietly buy the ubiquitous L.L. Bean backpacks for poorer kids who didn't have them. One secret gift, spilled to the press years later by former governor Angus King, was sending Christmas gifts and food to poorer families in Knox and Waldo counties.

In the public arena, perhaps the most stunning beneficence came when the K–8 Lincolnville Central School had to close suddenly due to mold problems. The state would build a new school on the site, but where would classes be held until then?

MBNA stepped in and built a school—in 54 days—on the grounds of its retreat center on Ducktrap Mountain, a building that most area towns would trade their schools for in a heartbeat.

Any attempt at quantifying the economic impact or listing the donations is doomed to fail. But ten years later, it's a story that needs to be told.

I was a reporter and editor in Belfast, Rockport, and Rockland during those years, and as I think back, it seems like a dream—a vision of a train roaring through, stopping long enough for gifts to tumble out. On a July morning in 2005, it was over.

For we journalists in the Midcoast, MBNA also was a gift that kept on giving. Each announcement—a new profits peak, more jobs, new buildings, six-figure donations—left us shaking our heads in wonder. And it was good news, not the dreary reporting of a plant closing. The towns in which we lived and were raising our children were made better, with new or improved schools, parks, libraries, and on and on.

≈

There were critics, of course; there was a dark side, and drama and conflict followed as a large national corporation tried to settle into small New England villages.

Critics claimed MBNA bullied the local newspapers. They said the nature of the business—lending through credit cards—hurt people, and society as a whole. The jobs paid well and the offices were far from the shoe and fish factories of the past, but many observed that the high-pressure phone sales were more like piecework than not.

Cawley was generous, but he wore his heart on his sleeve, and when his gifts and expansions were questioned or opposed, he was hurt, and that hurt sometimes led to anger. Plans to grow in Camden were rebuffed by many, and it seemed that Cawley responded by angrily shunning Camden for Belfast, where the company's presence would grow to 2,500 jobs.

Later, Cawley would say he understood the trepidation about the rapid growth in Camden; more community input was sought for an expansion in Rockland. With less fuss, call centers were opened in college towns like Brunswick, Farmington, Fort Kent, Presque Isle, and Orono.

The conspicuousness of the company's spending—like buying a small house, fixing it up, and then tearing it down—rankled many a Yankee's frugal values, and the yachts, private jets, and large black SUVs enjoyed by top management also seemed to be consciously flaunted.

The dramatic arc that became a pattern for MBNA was established early on. Flipping through the pages of the *Camden Herald* at the Walsh History Center at the Camden Public Library—the first established through MBNA largesse, the second, greatly expanded by it—the beginnings of the story unfold.

The January 23, 1993, issue reports that MBNA officials toured several possible office locations. The company would create 70 to 100 jobs, "a good fit for the town," a local architect told the paper.

On February 11, the news was that new offices would open on June 1, with 50 to 60 jobs, growing to 150. A company vice president noted that Camden was not unknown to senior managers. "MBNA has been holding management meetings here for over ten years," Richard Struthers said.

The March 4, 1993, *Herald* announced that MBNA would match funds of up to $250,000 for a local group restoring the Camden Opera House. This, just over a month after announcing its expansion in Maine, and before a single paycheck had been issued. The initial restoration budget had been $125,000; now, much more was possible, and indeed, the opera house was remade into the stunning venue it is today.

The story notes that MBNA "has expressed the hope that their contribution will confer a lasting benefit on the Midcoast area."

The company planned to lease part of a former mill, but in the April 29 paper, the headline told the tale: "A New Era—MBNA Purchases the Knox Mill," all 106,000 square feet of it.

The management retreats in Camden were not coincidental. Cawley's grandfather had lived in Lincolnville, and run clothing businesses in Belfast and Camden.

Those Camden roots are part of an oft-told story. As a young man, Cawley was returning to college and needed new tires on his car, but was unable to afford them. Camden's Bob Oxton, who apparently operated an auto shop, gave Cawley the tires, allowing the payment to follow.

Now, Cawley could repay Oxton more substantively, hiring him to help with the new building. Some saw a conflict of interest in Oxton, the town's fire chief, moonlighting for a private company that owned the biggest building in town. An editorial in the May 6 paper defended Oxton and the hiring, and the fuss was over.

In fewer than four months, the pattern was set: an expansion, jobs, more jobs than originally planned, a building purchase beyond what was planned, a high-profile donation, controversy, resolution. It would continue to play out elsewhere.

In retrospect, the company—which already had offices around the United States when it came to Maine—rode the tide of a booming economy through the late 1990s. Profits cracked the $1 billion mark in 1999; a year later it was $1.3 billion, then $1.7 billion in 2001, and $2.3 billion in 2003. Expansions in the UK, Ireland, and Spain followed.

Company officials regularly reported that its Maine offices performed better than others around the country. Cawley built a waterfront summer home in Camden. (In 1999, he hosted a fund-raiser for then-candidate George W. Bush at the house; former president George H. W. Bush was a guest at several MBNA events in Maine; and Cawley and his top executives were among the biggest donors to Republican campaigns.)

Describing itself as a bank without a lobby, MBNA

Celebrating the opening of Waterman's Community Center on North Haven
PETER RALSTON

was a cast-off division of Maryland Bank that Cawley and others took over and built around what they called *affinity marketing*. Credit cards with organization logos were issued to college alumni groups, professional associations, and other such groups. A portion of the purchases went to the groups, thereby ensuring they would promote their use.

≈

Cawley has been quoted as saying his goal was to give away his wealth, and he certainly gave a lot of it away. As CEO, he imbued the company with that same ethic. MBNA's generosity would be seen across a host of arenas. After the Camden Opera House, the company in 1994 donated $1 million to Penobscot Bay Healthcare, but education and the arts were major themes. Some of the bigger-ticket donations helped to renovate and expand the Rockland Public Library, the Camden Public Library (Barbara Bush appeared at the ribbon-cutting ceremony), and the Belfast Free Library.

The MBNA Foundation, Cawley, or both also paid to expand the Farnsworth Art Museum in Rockland, building the Jamien Morehouse Wing, named for Island Institute founder Philip Conkling's late wife, and turned an old church into the museum's Wyeth Center. They helped pay for Belfast's first YMCA building, and to expand Camden's into a regional facility.

On the islands, the company donated to North Haven's effort to create Waterman's Community Center, and was a major source of funding for the renovated and expanded Vinalhaven school. It helped to fund the purchase of seven miles of shoreline on Frenchboro, as well as improvements to the school, library, historical society, church, and parsonage. It gave grants to 13 island libraries.

"Charlie Cawley was on every nonprofit's radar in Maine, and particularly in the Midcoast," Conkling remembers. "Everybody wanted to talk to Charlie."

In the fall of 1999, Conkling and Institute cofounder Peter Ralston booked a meeting with him and explained the needs on year-round islands. Cawley wanted to see

Barbara Bush, left, and Elizabeth Moran at the ribbon-cutting ceremony for the Camden Public Library
COURTESY CAMDEN HERALD / ELIZABETH MORAN

the islands, and proposed visits to Frenchboro and Swan's Island.

"Little did we know this was going to be a tour in a helicopter," Conkling remembered, chuckling. On Frenchboro, "We take Charlie up to see the one-room schoolhouse," and from the small bookshelf that passed for the school library at the time, Cawley "pulled out a science reference book, published in 1964, that mentioned man going to the moon someday."

Cawley made an immediate decision, saying, "'I'm going to start an island library program,'" Conkling remembered.

The donations dramatically impacted not only island libraries, but also school and cultural enrichment programs, he said. On Vinalhaven, the state paid for a new

Frenchboro School students on Dr. Seuss's birthday
LUCAS MILARDO

school, but would fund only a shared library for the K–12 students. To build a better library, MBNA agreed to match up to the $1 million raised locally, and did.

"Nobody in Midcoast Maine had seen that kind of grantsmanship," Conkling said.

The company also funded the start of the Island Fellows program.

And then came a gift for the Institute. Conkling remembers a late-night call from Cawley, who said a sales agreement on the former Senter-Crane department store in Rockland would expire the next day. Did Conkling want it?

Despite the myriad concerns that raced through his brain, Conkling said a voice inside told him "Just say yes," and he did. The new building, sold to the Institute for $1, "truly put us on the map," allowing the growing staff room to work, and providing space for Archipelago, the store

and fine arts gallery, on Main Street.

One of the most profound impacts MBNA had was through the hundreds of college scholarships it awarded to students in Knox and Waldo counties. Later, the company included students in nine island communities in Hancock and Cumberland counties. Now, long after the corporate jets have left, those young men and women carry their education throughout their lives.

$\sim$

Before joining the Belfast *Republican Journal* newspaper, I worked for a social service agency in town, doing job training. A chicken-processing plant, sardine cannery, shoe factory, and french-fry processor were among the big employers. Some of those who came to our office for help were women who had developed carpal tunnel syndrome from cutting sardines with scissors, day in, day out, or who suffered bouts of "chicken poisoning," some kind of bacteria that took hold in the cracks in their hands.

Flash forward to 1995, when MBNA executive Shane Flynn was giving me a tour of the beautiful new Belfast office. I heard several women's voices calling out, "Hi, Tom!" I recognized them as the same former factory workers. Instead of cold, wet, noisy conditions, they now worked in a climate-controlled office, sitting comfortably in their cubicles.

Another personal note: As someone who loves his adopted hometown of Belfast, I am regularly reminded of MBNA each time I walk or drive along the waterfront. When the sprawling concrete chicken plant that dominated much of the waterfront went belly-up in 1988, it sat vacant—covered in graffiti, decrepit and smelly—for almost ten years. City government talked about getting rid of it, but nothing was done.

MBNA purchased the property with the idea of building offices there, where its yachts could dock, but instead, Cawley decided to build a park for the city.

Years later, Front Street Shipyard revived the other end of the waterfront, but I believe if that park had not been built, a business like the shipyard would have looked elsewhere.

In July 2005, while reporting for the *Bangor Daily News*, I learned that Bank of America would be buying MBNA. On a conference call that included questions from the *Wall Street Journal*, *LA Times*, and CNBC, I was surprised to hear my name called. I asked Cawley's successor at MBNA what he would say to those workers arriving at the Belfast office that morning when they learned of the sale. He said that if nothing had been done, there would be no more MBNA. The company, other sources said, had resisted diversifying into home mortgages and insurance, and risked running out of new markets for its credit-card lending.

Today, there is no more MBNA. But the legacy remains.

Angus King, now a US senator, was Maine's governor during those years. When the company was bought, he summed up what it meant: "If I had sat down in 1994 with a blank sheet of paper and written down the ideal company for Maine," he said, "it would have been MBNA." ♦

Tom Groening is editor of Island Journal *and* The Working Waterfront.

The Harbor Walk at Steamboat Landing in Belfast, site of the former chicken plant
TOM GROENING

Islands in Time Society

Gift Planning at the Island Institute

Members of the Islands in Time Society are committed to making a difference in Maine's year-round island and remote coastal communities for generations to come. Through thoughtful planning and designation of bequests, trusts, annuities, and life insurance, members craft gifts of lasting significance.

We invite you to join, and we thank our members who have chosen to make a remarkable investment in our work.

To learn more about the benefits of gift planning, contact Michelle Smith, Donor Relations Director, at msmith@islandinstitute.org or (207) 594-9209 ext. 138.

Members

Charles Beran
John and Mary Alice Bird
Nancy McLeod Carter
Margery S. Foster
Rosalind S. Holt
Ellen V. Howe
Philip and Ann Lape
Virginia B. Lloyd
Emily Lansingh Muir
Elizabeth B. Noyce
Anne P. Owsley
Molly Potter Scheu
George and Anna Shaw
Margaret L. Snow
Richard Stephenson
John and Martha Stewart
Willoughby T. Stuart
Charles O. Verrill, Jr.
H. Jeremy Wintersteen
Frances B. Youngblood

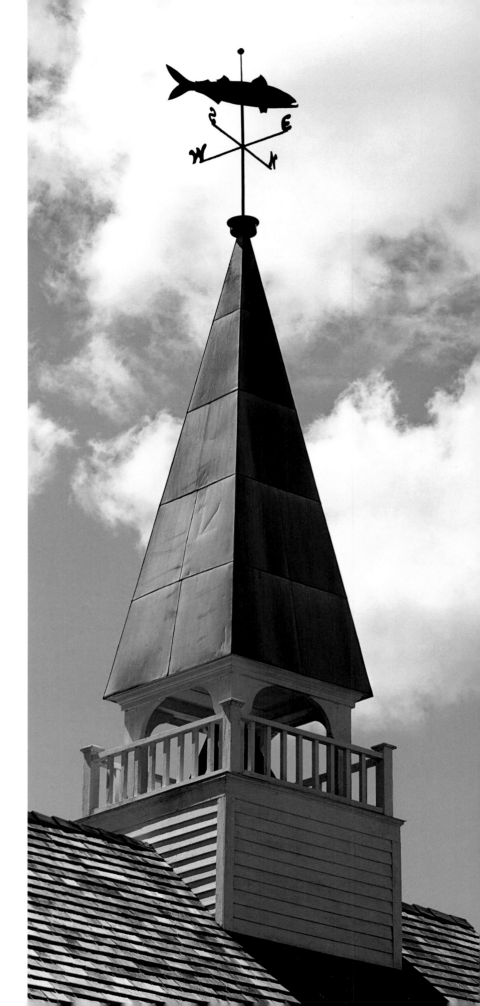